BECOMING RUTH

Copyright 2022 John Burns

All rights reserved.

ISBN: 979-8-4139395-4-3

All rights reserved. Non-commercial interests may reproduce portions of this book without the express written permission of the author, provided the text does not exceed 500 words. When reproducing text from this book, include the following credit line: "Becoming Ruth by John Burns. Used by permission."

Commercial interests: No part of this publication may be reproduced in any form, stored in a retrieval system, or transmitted in any form by any means - electronic, photocopy, recording, or otherwise - without prior written permission of the publisher, except as provided by the United States of America copyright law.

BECOMING RUTH

THE GENTILE BRIDE OF THE KINSMAN REDEEMER

John Burns

Dedication

To the men of Task Force Ranger and Bravo Company 3/75 Ranger Regiment.

To Jesus Christ for saving me from myself.

Table of Contents

Preface...7

MERCY

My Struggle..11
The Gulf War...22
The Valley of Elah... 35
Can America Police Itself.............................. 45
PTSD Answer... 53
Parenting Perversion..................................... 66
Deification of the Woman..............................76
American Naivete... 90
The Ephesian Dilemma 104
Biblical Tithing...111
Jezreel.. 120
Learn the Parable of the Fig Tree............... 130

GRACE

Socrates Once Quipped................................145
Losing a Friend..162

Table of Contents

Practicing Synecretism 177
How to Understand the Bible 187
Who is this Jonah son of Ammitai 197
A Modern Tale of Two Cities 214
Humble Pie 225
The Tabernacle 240
The Architecture of Ruth 253
The Mark of Cain 271
The Two-Edged Sword 278
Into the Breach 284
Special Operations Wounded Warriors 293
Biography 302

Preface

In the annals of history, many men have set down to understand the truths of the Bible. This is one chapter in my life, where God took me behind the veil of eternity to teach the paradigm of Levirite marriage and gentile brides that litter the pages of our Old Testament.

God promised Adam that the seed of the serpent would bruise his head, and the seed of the woman would bruise the heel. This is a conundrum for women have no seed. God always intended to become the promised seed that would redeem creation from its curse.

From Adam to Messiah is a complete bloodline. Do you realize that there were gentile brides contained in the bloodline of Messiah? This is a biblical prose hidden in the text pointing to Messiah receiving a gentile bride from all the nations of the earth, during the Church age.

Ruth is our shining example for what it takes to earn the hand of our kinsman redeemer, Jesus Christ.

She has endured much heartache. Every man she knows is dead and she is a widow in a world where men inherited everything. Her future looked bleak. Praise God she took the road less traveled.

Ruth is an incredible story, when prayer and thanksgiving are offered, and we lose our religious pre-suppositions, we allow the Holy Spirit to teach us what God alone intends us to learn.

If you are looking for a female role model in this life, become the Ruth of the Bible. Her humility in serving the God of her adoptive family is the pattern God established when we accept Jesus Christ's offer of marriage. We agree to serve the God of Israel! Our Kinsman redeemer is Yeshua Ha Messiah.

He was crucified upon a cross of wood, yet he created the hill upon which it stood.

Enjoy Becoming Ruth.

MERCY

My Struggle

With the gift of hindsight, if I could change anything about my life, would I change anything? With the command by Christ to redeem the time, would I change anything about my life?

In my early life, divorce, foster care, grand- parents stepping in to help raise two children caught in the middle of the American phenomenon of single parent households, are how my developmental years began. Train up a child in the way they should go, and when they are old, they will not depart from it.

This applies to ungodly things as well as Godly things. The seeds of divorce were planted in my life when I was 18 months of age. I would never see my biological mother again, until I was 47 years old. How-ever, as a Messianic Christian, I am thankful I went through it, for my sanctification alone is in the knowledge that I am saved.

After my parents separated, I was raised in my fathers' parent's home, until I was 4 1/2 years old, and my father remarried. It was a Roman Catholic upbringing, accompanied by a strong, patriotic fervor on every American holiday. I would learn of my grandfather's service in World War 2 and my stepmothers fathers service as a Marine in Chesty Pullers storied 7th Marine Regiment.

A normal American childhood for most Roman Catholics, however I always felt there was more to my story. Those thoughts were confirmed when I visited my grandparents on my biological mothers' side of the family.

I was prepared by my grandmother to understand that they were Polish Catholics who emigrated to America in the 20's. When I arrived at their House in New Jersey My sister and I were introduced to Olga and Milton Luster. My Polish grandmother was making Kielbasa and I sat down to talk with my grandfather. He was mixing English with his native tongue, and I began to enquire about certain items in his modest home.

He had a lampstand made of bronze with seven distinct candle sticks. And, he had a blue and white prayer shawl with tassels, and, writing that I would not recognize until I began to study languages while serving in the military. One thing I carried through my catholic upbringing was the knowledge that none of my other friends or families that were catholic had those items anywhere in their homes. So, I carried the intuition that one day I would learn what those items rightly identified were. I never forgot.

My family eventually settled in Briarcliffe, a small enclave of white working- class Americans. Irish, Italian, German, Polish, and, every other European second- generation immigrant's families. Nearly every kid in the neighborhood went to a Catholic school. I attended Catholic school through tenth grade.

High school is where I began to rebel tremendously against the external morality taught by priests, nuns, and lay teachers. Catholic Catechism was incredibly confusing, so in sixth grade I began to read my Father's vulgate, and in the births section is where I learned my mother and father had lost a child in 1968.

It led to the turmoil in my mother's heart that led her to use Valium, and Methamphetamine, eventually leading to her leaving my father while he attended basic training in Louisiana.

My mother placed my sister and I in foster care, and my dad ended up leaving the military with an extreme hardship discharge. My father, with two young children, and a young wife, did not shirk his responsibility to answer his draft notice. He attempted to become part of the true 1 percent of Americans who have actually served our country in a time of War.

I admire my father for accepting every challenge life has thrown his way and, for giving me a safe home to lay my head down in every night.

My life in Briarcliffe was one of Catholic school life, with sports to keep us busy while my father worked, and my stepmother raised four children in a three-bedroom rowhome. Growing up in the neighborhood meant drugs, older kids trying them, and alcohol easily purchased. This changed my high school experience.

I dropped out of Catholic high school to attend a recently desegregated public school. I cut class, smoked dope, and had sex often with girls more than willing to cut school with me.

I got a Job finishing concrete, and doing every type of masonry known. It promoted an incredible lifelong work ethic in me but I was terrible at managing money. I spent every penny I earned in local bars and buying drugs to include cocaine, methamphetamine, and eventually heroine. All by the age of eighteen.

My taste for narcotics would haunt me through the rest of my life. Somehow, at seventeen, I managed to walk into an Army recruiter's office. Without any knowledge of the job's the military offered, I accepted my fate, and enlisted in the Army reserves with a May 1985 date for basic training. I was assigned to an Army reserve unit on Wissahickon Avenue. We drilled locally one weekend a month, and I attended an annual training exercise in Fort Pickett in Blackstone Virginia.

I tried to reenroll in school which lasted only six months before quitting to get my GED, and continue working. My narcotics habit progressed to heroine, and eventually I enlisted in the Army to escape my Philadelphia surroundings. You can run from drugs, but they will find you.

I reported to Fort Ord in California on 23 September 1987 and the 1st Battalion, 9th Infantry as Private Burns. I had found the structure my life needed for growth. I began to impress my leaders and they rewarded me with increased responsibility. A chance encounter while supporting a sister infantry battalion in a training exercise changed my military life forever.

I was asked to drive for the 4th BN. 21st infantry Scout platoon at the National training center in Southern California. I was assigned to SSG John Harrison. He had a yellow star on his jump wings, and he wore the coveted 1st Bn 75th Infantry Airborne Ranger scroll, designating his jump into Grenada in 1983. I wanted to be a Ranger and serve in the 75th Infantry.

As I communicated my intentions to my Squad leader, it fueled resentment and jealousy. He vowed to accel and go to Ranger school first. He got his chance, and blew it. He failed the entrance PT test. I asked my platoon Sergeant if I could take the test the following day. I did, and I passed the PT test and swim test. Then my Bn commander took a chance, and allowed me to go to pre ranger as a Pfc 11c Infantryman with no experience with the Ranger Handbook. I would not let him down.

I reported to Combat leadership course in October 1988. My instructor is a man I would befriend for the rest of my life. Jose Gordon was also a Grenada Raider. He took me under his wing. I somehow graduated from the hardest school I

My Struggle

had ever tried. This put me on a short list to attend Ranger school at Fort Benning Georgia,

I would report to Ranger school in June of 1989. I reported to 4th Ranger Training Bn. And was assigned to Charlie company 1st platoon. I was placed in a squad of fellow enlisted personnel, all from the Ranger Regiment. I became Ranger buddies with my lifelong best friend Paul Mercer. He would end up saving me many times in Ranger school. I flat out did not have the experience he had in daily ranger life, and he had the patience to somehow get us both through.

I graduated in August 1989 with every intention of reenlisting and going to serve in the Regiment. Upon my return to Fort Ord, I would run into Sgt. Gordon at the PX and, show him my newly acquired tab. He had reenlisted to return to 1st Bn. And I told him I was going to reenlist in December 1989 when I became eligible, and report to the Regiment. Both of our lives would collide in the invasion of Panama.

Operation Just Cause saw me deploy to Panama in December and he would Jump again with 1st Bn., on Torrijos Tocumen Airport.

I would reenlist in Panama, and Go to the promotion board in January. I would report to Fort Benning permanently to begin Airborne school, and attend ROP with I month as an NCO. My life would never again be slow!

Upon ROP Graduation I was assigned to 3d Bn. As an 11c2v. I reported to the personnel building, and met SSG Gene Potocki. He would be my Platoon Sergeant, and

Mikey Collins would be my section Sergeant. I would report to the Company 1sg. In the Morning. and my first day in Bravo company ended with an invitation to go drinking at a Strip Joint with members of my platoon. I fell prey to their supplying endless shots of Tequila while they themselves drank water.

I somehow was transported back to B company, and on my first morning I missed formation. Luckily the company went to watch two members of Bravo company begin the Best Ranger Competition and I was allowed to sleep in.

At 0900 the door of the room I was in flew open and I was asked to report to the 1sg. Sitting in that office were all four Platoon sergeants. They all had jumped into Panama and I had deployed there with the 7th Division. 1sg. Took an immediate disliking to my combat patch, and immediately told me anyone with a combat scroll could effectively smoke me regardless of their rank. I spent the next Year learning to respect the spec4 mafia and the NCOs in Bn. who had gone before me. I would have to prove I was cut from their cloth by action, not patches or words.

My first chance came during Regimental command inspection. My roommate was Sgt. (P) Daniel D. Busch. He was an amazing Ranger, and an even better man. For the next two years Dan would teach me so much about existing in Bn., and the entire mentality based upon respect for ability. I would get my first chance to prove I had the mental aptitude for Bn. life during regimental command inspection 1990, when CSM Leon Guerero entered our room with the 1sg, and SSG Potocki, and SFC Dietrich.

We stood at parade rest as the CSM inspected our uniform and our billet room for cleanliness. Upon entering our shared NCO latrine, the CSM asked us to enter behind him. As he lifted the toilet seat revealing a brown object stuck to the porcelain, when he asked Dan and I to explain what the object was: So, I reached into the bowl with my finger, scraped it off, tasted it, and replied "It taste like shit CSM!"

For one split second I saw my Ranger career end; and then everybody burst out in laughter, and SFC Dietrich actually laughed, and shook my hand. It would begin a friendship that would last until I deployed to Somalia from Texas, and the last person I would say goodbye to in the Regiment was 1sg Dietrich now back in 2d Ranger Bn. I confided in him where we were going, and he replied" your job is to lead Rangers".

I knew then that somehow three years of hard training and harder living would mean I had to now come good on the Ranger creed. The standard set in the regiment by 1SG Dietrich is one of legend amongst Rangers who served with him. I admire him to this day. My prayer is that I will see Deke at a Ranger reunion or at least in Heaven.

1993 began with myself and Dan taking different paths as now SSG's in 3d Bn. Dan had attended Selection and I would compete in Best Ranger in May. Dan had succeeded, and I would come up short in the competition. I was not ready for the competition, and had nagging ankle injury incurred while training for the spot jump two weeks before the competition. No excuses. I tried and came up short.

1993 would also see a leadership change in 3d bn. We had an unfortunate accident in the fall of 1992. I had returned from Malaysian survival school, and was asked to report to Bn. headquarters to brief LTC Keneally about the need for Ranger NCOs to attend this particular school.

He was an incredibly approachable and humble man. I entered his office as he was packing to leave for Savannah to evaluate the 1st Bn. Commander in Utah on a Bn. training mission. He had me sit down, and then proceeded to ask me about my men and if they have everything to get the Ranger mission done if called upon. I felt honored that a Bn. Commander was worried about my Squad with 35 other squads in the Bn. He genuinely understood that his success was dependent upon the success of every Ranger under his command. That is Ranger Brotherhood!

No human should ever build a house upon a bad foundation. The Ranger foundation runs deep. It was forged in the fire of combat, and continued in the billows of hard training every single day. America is in good hands when the Regiment remembers it's historical foundations.

The Ranger squad is the individual cell that binds with every other Ranger squad, and support personnel to form the Ranger DNA sequence. But, at the heart of Ranger success, is the Ranger rifleman, grenadier, saw gunner, team leaders, and squad leader.

My Struggle

No Ranger is more important than his subordinates. The commanders get in trouble when they think the Regt. runs because of them!

LTC Keneally left for Savannah. I knew not that the salute I rendered would be our last in this body.

Over the weekend we were alerted and, I reported to B company to learn devastating news that would affect every Ranger in 3d bn. A Helicopter had crashed in the salt flats of Utah killing both Bn. Commanders, and, Harvey Moore the winner of the Inaugural best Ranger competition. The Ranger community was devastated.

I remember seeing the S3 Major Ron Russell visibly Shaken as he had to deliver the news to our wounded Bn. It affected me on into my later years but, I found solace when I chose to visit LTC Keneally's grave in Arlington after I was wounded in Somalia and spent a month in D.C.

On the back of his tombstone are incredible words of wisdom. "It is not the destination that counts, but the journey you take along the way." That sums up the Christian man's heart, and was a final leadership challenge to future generations of Rangers.

Today as Rangers fight in a protracted war, they are returning to a confused America in the middle of a moral identity crisis. Rangers more than ever need to not isolate and be alone. Nothing is more important than spending time with the Rangers you served with in peace and war. We have an unbroken DNA chain. It is the common blood type of the regimental Ranger. A gift from the intelligent designer of the universe. God loves Rangers! He wants Rangers to understand his plan for mankind. It is the most preposterous debt payment plan in Human History.

He does not need any more three- dimensional spaces called Church. He needs you to understand his plan is grounded in his love for his creation, with us as the centerpiece of the cosmic love story called the Word of God. It is a two- edged sword, and contains your DNA, and owners- manual, and your life's warranty deed.

Surrender is a Ranger word: But only when surrender involves accepting Jesus Christ death as payment for our sin debt to God the Father. We all owe it. It can only be paid by believing Jesus Christ Died for you. Born once die twice. Born twice die once! Hallelujah.

LTC Keneally will greet me alongside Daniel D. Busch, and they both shall receive the soul winners crown for leading me to a saving relationship with the Christ. He was crucified on a cross of wood, yet he created the hill upon which it stood!

Even so come Lord Jesus Christ.

RLTW John Burns.

The Gulf War

Most Americans today could not tell you that America invaded Iraq in 1991. George H.W. Bush was President, and Saddam Hussein had invaded Kuwait. America had incredible interest in the gulf region. The Bush Legacy is one of jobs unfinished.

America invaded Panama in 1989. We deposed a dictator who was no longer a convenient tool of the CIA that President Bush once ran and modernized. The Bush years at the CIA post World War 2 are one where the United States replaces any leader, of any country, at any time, to fit the American governments foreign policy agenda.

At last count, the CIA that George H W Bush created, is one where American foreign policy required the toppling of a country every few years.

Chile, Nicaragua, Panama, Argentina, Iraq, Iran, Syria, Libya, Egypt, Yemen and on, and on, and on. The culture he created is one of modern American political eugenics at work. According to him, the greatness of America was one where we project power by replacing people we do not agree with.

He exercised his will not God's perfect will. He believed in the God of fortresses, and projecting American military might is what kept America great. I completely disagree!

George H.W. Bush was labeled a War hero after WW2. I have no problem with humans elevating people to a position of hero after wartime exploits. My problem is with people who never have exchanged gunfire with an enemy of America, then you should leave heroism to warfighters to determine if a man rises to the level of hero.

A President who is a hero will serve God first. Going to church has nothing to do with serving God. Shema Israel Adonai Elohim Echad Adonai! The Lord our God is one God, and he gave us the Bible to teach gentile leaders how to properly govern from a Godly biblical perspective.

No President should engage in entering treaties with the enemies of God's people, or with those who attack his Messiah and plan. The United Nations has only ever been truly united, when it unites to stop what God is accomplishing in Israel.

President Bush had no right to back the United Nations from a Biblical perspective. The UN is united to stop Israel from uniting their land and building the millennial temple for Yeshua to return to.

The United Nations will commit political suicide to stop Israel, and Jesus Christ at any cost. And, he left The Gulf in worse shape than before Saddam invaded Kuwait.

God let the Presidency of George H.W. Bush collapse, and he allowed America to elect a smooth talking, southern politician with a wife bent on sowing death, hell and the grave in America. Clinton was raised in the eugenic southern Baptist convention. His wife never knew God. Her goal is the deification of the woman, the murder of the unborn, and the euthanasia of the nation of Israel at all costs.

Ahab and Jezebel invaded the White House. Bill Clinton raped a Jewish princess, while his wife began her career murdering Vince Foster over a real estate deal, just like Jezebel. Her goal has always been the erosion of the values upon which our country was founded.

The Puritans won our revolution, they wrote our Constitution, and bill of rights, and they built our economy, while they fought in every war America has waged. They did it all, while protecting God's Jewish remnant for the time we are now living in. It will take puritans to rightly divide the word of truth and it takes sons of Issachar to unveil the times as they pertain to Israel.

Bill Clinton negotiated with every middle eastern leader but the Jewish remnant. He was a terrible president no matter how he handled the economy, God's people rely only on him for their needs if they truly are his people.

The two golden calves set up by Jeroboam, were worshipped by Bill Clinton. For a draft dodger who would not die for his liberal political beliefs, he sure was willing to let me die for mine, and his. 9/11, was the harbinger that led to George W. Bush.

Interestingly, the closest he ever came to serving our country is one picture of him in a flight suit. Privilege is on full display with George W. Bush. History was thrust upon him, and he did what his father did: not finish the job. He negotiated with every Muslim leader that God abhorred. He Invaded Iraq and left it in worse shape with Shia majority rule being a puppet of the Iranian Regime.

He may have gotten the Saddam Hussein dynasty executed, but what has America gained?

A 600- Million- dollar Embassy in BABYLON! It will be destroyed when a nuclear exchange finally hits the Sunni-Shia Schism, and we are right in the middle. I pray Biden gets the 3 trillion in oil they owe us before they decide to kill each other over Israel and God's perfect will for their lives. Where the Carcas's lie, there the eagles will be gathered.

Every nation with an eagle as an emblem, will one day unite to try and stop God's plan of redemption of his tithe of land, Israel and his people. To include the bald eagle of America.

One day an American President will cross God! He will turn the eagle on our presidential seal away from the olive branch of Israel, and toward the arrows of war. He will unite the Satanic trinity of Pope in Rome with an Assyrian dictator and an American president.

We are on the cusp God's crescendo and Trump was America's judge. Joe Biden will unite the Satanic Trinity under the banner of Anti-Christ.

9/11 made us more arrogant than ever. 20- year protracted fight against an ideology that now enjoys more immigration rights to America than before we were attacked by Muslims.

Barak Obama was friend of everything Arab and everything Muslim. Black liberation theology became the rallying cry post assassination of black America's prophet. With the death of Dr. King, only charlatan, millionaire, Caucasian-haters, fought for black Americans, and I fear we are more divided than ever.

To judge only by skin color is exactly what Dr. King warned us of he did not want. Today race baiters try to convince us, that there is more than one race of humans. Noah had three sons by one wife. That is what made him righteous before God. His DNA was still perfect, and his sons married the daughters of men who had not lain with the fallen angels. He produced the human race that we are all descended from. One black son, One Asian Son, and one gentile white son.

These three sons of Noah repopulated the entire earth, and we are all descended from some combination of all three.

You can find your ancestors from examining the table of nations that descend from Ham, Shem, and Japheth. Race should never be how we examine each other. All have sinned and fall short of the glory of God. We all need God's grace and mercy every day.

The Politicians that produced the Bush's, The Mccain's, the Clintons, the Cheney's, Mc Connell, Schumer, all have a lot to lose. The State Department has become a de facto way for them to project power to fit their Muslim globalist agenda. Donald Trump understands that he needed to drain the swamp of D.C. for our nation to survive.

They have a lot to lose. Power is something neither side will cede by election ever again. American voters became irrelevant. The lengths the corrupt Obama administration went to destroy Mike Flynn is treasonous. He was the one guy the law required to be briefed on any investigations into the incoming Trump administration that Barak and Hillary Clinton had labeled as deplorables.

They knew, Donald J. Trump would upset the apple cart they have been harvesting.

Our system can guarantee nothing but corruption. Bankruptcy is the only thing that will reset our American political debacle. Both sides are completely corrupt. They will only ever unite when an outsider who is poor comes out of the woodwork to challenge how they see us.

I love America. I do not like Americans! They are purveyors of everything God abhors! They have become completely apathetic. It is not a problem that they do not know this, it becomes a problem when you stop caring that you do not know! Americans have voted in two parties that have none of the common man's interests in mind.

If you are a heterosexual working man who attends Church with his family, then you are the enemy of the American government. If you are a recruiter for the homosexual community, you become an advisor to Presidents.

If you believe in race baiting rather than spending time with people you do not look like, you are part of our American problem. I do not need to be told a black man is black or I am white. I can see. I take people one at a time. If you are for Jesus Christ, I am for you.

America is at a crossroads. We had a President actually doing things God agrees with. He is the only candidate that can actually help us emerge from financial bankruptcy. He has done it several times in his successful real estate empire. The current crop of career politicians got us here. They have been on a spending spree, and each successive administration has kicked the ball to the next administration. What changed with Trump?

America has gotten so use to electing men who look great on the outside. Polished, polite and completely incompetent in governance. Lobby purchased and American indoctrinated charlatans interested in only themselves. America needed a narcissist! When the number one photo in every grandmother's home becomes a selfie, we got to look inside ourselves.

When we have an overwhelming sense of wanting to be entertained then why do they get mad when an entertainer is elected President? Because they have been unmasked. Trump has inspired me to write. America has to Listen. This Global pandemic is from God! He allowed it to chasten us home to sound biblical reasoning. It is his pattern since he put us in the garden. He loves us and he wants us to know he is in charge ,and his will is playing out and neither side gave Trump a fair chance.

Never in American history have people united to take down a dually elected President. Their agenda is complete lawlessness. Abortion, Homosexual rights, destruction of the values that made America great.

Racism disguised as civil rights. Islamism. You may not want Christ but I promise you do not want Islam and their Mahdi! Trump was halting the advance of Islam into America in favor of Biblical Zionism. Every Christian should have given Trump their vote, for he was restoring God to a place of worship in America. I fear it may be our last chance at redemption before his attention turns eastward again!

Our obsession with capitalism will begin the downfall of America. Any form of government to replace it will only serve to replace God wholly in our lives. Government as God is the agenda of every politician elected to federal office. No party has God's true interests in mind. If they did, a President would have already had the courage to recognize Jerusalem as Jesus Christ eternal, capital city.

No republican had the courage to stop the euthanasia of Black Babies in the womb like Donald J. Trump. Not even Black President Obama stopped killing black babies or stopped incarcerating black men at extraordinary rates based upon the democratic agenda. Political eugenics carried out upon a population in the name of progress. A progressive will never stop these practices and we are progressing toward complete immorality and lawlessness.

Donald J. Trump scares the career politicians because he believes in the Bill of Rights. He believes in limited government. He believes in deregulation. He believes in fighting for every American citizen and he believes in fighting the non- Americans occupying offices in DC, disguised as representatives of the people, and, in fighting the people who continue to elect them.

None of these people has followed George Washington's example, and every one of them would happily be crowned king if you let them. They crave power and money more than anything. Quit electing ungodly representatives if you believe in Yeshua Ha Messiah. Find out which leaders God chose in the pages of your Old Testament.

King David is where I start and finish. He is God's man. He was intemperate. He fought the enemies of Israel with incredible tenacity and determination. He took on the religious elite class. He took on the corrupt priests. He murdered Uriah, committed adultery with Bathsheba, placed usurper Solomon on the throne, and still God calls David a man after mine own heart in Acts 15, and, God is rebuilding David's earthly kingdom just like he promised Mary the mother of our Lord.

David served God's purposes even when his life did not fit all the hallmarks of a king that men think are better than God's Man. David is completely flawed, and God continues to use him today, Hallelujah he alone is God.

America had better get used to Donald Trump. God is exonerating him even if he does not know it. The Bush's, the Clintons, the Obama's will all fall in the wake of Donald Trump and not because of Trump, but because he was doing God's bidding. America needed a chastening and God chose Trump to put us back on God's agenda.

If you do not believe me, I am not your problem. Biblical literacy is your problem. Any morality or Church tradition that is not in the Bible will be destroyed before Jesus Christ sets up his kingdom in Jerusalem. I pray Trump would get us back on God's calendar. It is a 360- day Babylonian calendar. It revolves around Jewish holidays that Jesus Christ actually followed.

Passover, Feast of Firstfruit's, Pentecost, Feast of Dedication, Yom Kippur.

No Birthdays. No Funerals. No Memorial Day. No Easter, No Christmas.

The Sabbath is still Friday evening to Saturday evening. No more kidnapping of God for two Hours on pagan Sunday. The first day of God's work week, so church is work, and that is why the preacher demands wages. He has his reward! Jesus Christ will not be in the temple on Sunday and you better know the moon cycles!

The next year will see the final collapse of the American monetary system because we refuse to tear down the two golden calves of Jeroboam. The swamp of New York also needs draining. It is a modern Pergamos on the coast of Western Turkey. The seat of Satan on Earth.

The cult of Mithras that has mesmerized America during times of prosperity, will collapse. Corruption replaced fiduciary responsibility in America's financial institution boardrooms. Wall Street will collapse and the entire post

World War two Bretton Woods agreement will have to be renegotiated.

China will not lay by idly. Russia is already planning to take Middle East spoils. Donald Trump was dependent upon our monetary solvency and our military might: The two golden CALVES OF JEROBOAM!

America must return to God and his perfect will for their lives. Our political system is insolvent, and a Revolution is on our horizon. Teshuva! Repent and return to God the creator for all of your needs in this life. He alone is capable of meeting all of them. Accept his sacrifice for the payment of your sin debt.

Believe that Jesus Christ died to raise dead men to life. He is not in the business of making bad men good, that is what church and doctrine try to accomplish, God just saves sinners!

Donald Trump has many flaws from the external misfortune of being the American president. Good thing that God never judges by outward ability or inability. He looks at a man or woman's conviction to the accomplishment of Godly purposes. Trump was doing more to line up with the Bible, than any President in my lifetime of 52 years. Your problem is not with Trump it is with Gods' will for your life.

America Needed Donald Trump. Our President's had negotiated with the enemies of God for too many years running. Trade agreements saddled our Children's Children's Children's Children's Children,s Children's Children to tax burdens for the next three thousand years. My military retirement will never last, they already spent it on their un-American agenda.

Globalism is a Godly idea if the goal is preaching the death, burial, and resurrection of Jesus Christ. If missionary outreach is their goal, I am all in. But that is not the current American situation. Their goal, is to thwart the plan and agenda of God. If you vote for them, then you are voting to replace Jesus Christ as our Messiah.

Jesus Christ alone separated church and state when he washed his disciples' feet. Government will never wash anyone's feet! However, when Government attempts to right wrongs against God's will, we owe that government our vote.

The last thing I was praying for in November 2016 , was for Donald Trump to order the Attorney General to sue to have the Bible put back in public school, and prayer to return to the morning routine of children in public school.

School shootings will become a thing of the past. Children will have their weapons by which they wage spiritual warfare, and then alone will America be great again!

The Gulf War is still being fought. It is the Gulf between the holiness of God and our unrighteousness. It is an impassible gulf. Water alone can not bridge the gulf. Only the death of God himself could solve the sin question in each of our lives. The gulf is too great for religious conviction and doctrine to have any effect. It is a time issue, not a three- dimensional space issue.

God alone inhabits eternity, and, he wants you there. To get there, you must get on board with God's plan. It begins when you believe Jesus Christ died to pay your sin debt to God, and it meanders through life with daily Bible reading to know where we are in God's plan. Jesus Christ was crucified to solve your time issue. God redeems time when a sinner accepts Christ. Hallelujah!

He was crucified on a Cross of Wood Yet he Created the Hill upon which it stood!

Even so come Lord Jesus Christ.

RLTW John Burns 6-7-2021.

The Valley of Elah

Sticking with Hebrew hermeneutics, the law of first mention rightly applied, gives the transliteration of the word Elah. We first encounter the masculine proper name of Elah in the book of Genesis. Elah is one of the dukes born to Esau. Esau is the twin brother of Jacob.

Esau was Isaac's favorite. Isaac believed that his firstborn son, Esau would inherit all the promises God had given his father Abram. This included Isaac believing that he would be the father of the promised Messiah.

Rebekah was Esau and Jacob's mother. She would have spent her pregnancy dreaming of her male son inheriting the progenitor-ship of the Messianic line. When twins were born, confusion abounded in Isaac and Rebekahs' household.

Esau was the Firstborn. Jacob would spend his days as the second son of Isaac. Playing second fiddle was not the plan of Rebekah, and her son would somehow become the chosen son, if she had anything to do about it.

Isaac Loved Esau because he was a man's man. He was a hunter, and he provided food for his family. Jacob was a shepherd.

Isaac gave Esau the name because of his complexion, and his extremely hairy body. These traits permeate the Edomite community today in Israel.

Jacob would have to bear the name that transliterates as deceiver. If God could justify Jacob, he can justify you.

When the time came for Isaac to be gathered to God, Rebekah conspired to deceive her husband. She took advantage of her aging husband's blindness to deceive him into placing God's blessing on Jacob and not on Easu. Jacob went so far as to shear a sheep to pretend he was hairy Esau.

The pro-genitor- ship of Messiah is all a woman of Hebrew descent hope for. That is why God gave us Mary. Gods' woman would become the mother of Messiah, and the sins of Rebekah could be justified.

Why this elaborate hoax was allowed, only God knows why. Jacob received the promises given to Abraham, and Jacob would become the father of Judah, and his grandson David would become king over Israel. Mary would become the virgin mother of Jesus Christ, and the descendant of David. Hallelujah.

Esau would also be promised certain things. He would be the father of a great people. How-ever, the deception carried out by Jacob and Rebekah continues to haunt the relationship between Jacob and Esaus' descendant's today, and will finally culminate in the Psalm 83 war.

Edom as a territory survives, along with Moab and Ammon, further displaying God's eternal mercy upon his creation.

Esau would become the father of eleven offspring. Elah is one of those offspring. His name transliterates as an oak. The oak is one of the most amazing trees. It is dense and hard as woodpecker lips. Esau has the same traits as a people. Nothing but the blood of Jesus Christ will soften the stance of the Edomites in Israel. The relationship between Jacob and Israel is what eventually leads to the Armageddon war. Peace will only come to Israel when Jesus Christ returns to set up his eternal Kingdom in Jerusalem.

Edom is the territory that modern Jordan occupies. Jordan was born as a buffer state set up by the extremely Islamic leaning United Nations. It is a juvenile country with ancient foundations. Jordan is nothing more than a proxy country run by Arab Nationalist's bent on stopping God's plan for Israel and the entire world.

If Jordan can pretend to support peace while keeping its' people in bondage to the house of the moon god, they can stop the plans of God for placing Jesus Christ on the Davidic throne in Israel. Israel will be forced to confront Jordan militarily very soon. It is God's will. It will lead to the final chastening of God upon Israel for not knowing the time of the advent of God's messiah, the Lord Jesus Christ.

The valley of Elah is where David confronts Goliath. Goliath is the offspring of fallen angels and Canaanite women. He was a Nephillim. The Nephillim are the race of giants first mentioned in Genesis 6. It is the real reason God flooded the earth. God had promised to provide a Messiah born to a virgin Jewish woman. Lucifer deployed his angel mercenaries to block God's plan of redemption. He ordered the fallen angels to impregnate human women, and the race of giants was born.

God flooded the earth to destroy the plans of Satan and saved the offspring of men that had not polluted themselves with Nephillim perversion. The Sons of God went into the daughters of men. It is a subtlety you will not understand reading English translations of the Bible. You must understand Hebrew to understand the duality contained in the name of the Nephillim.

They enjoyed dual DNA. They will return as prophesied by Jesus Christ before he can return. I believe they will be involved in the Psalm 83 war that is on our near horizon.

David was anointed by Samuel to be Gods' man on the throne in Israel. He was born to adulterous parents. Jesse had six children by his wife. Psalm 51 alerts us to the fact that in iniquity David was born. His mother had been the wife of the king of Ammon. David would enjoy mixed relations with the Ammonites when he was king.

David was the seventh son born to Jesse. He was given the lowly job of being the family shepherd. God always uses shepherds to get his sheep to follow him unconditionally. Everyone was shocked when the man of God chose twelve -year- old David.

His brothers were all soldiers. How could God choose a shepherd rather than a soldier? What if David is a soldier disguised as a shepherd to confuse Satan? With the gift of hind-sight we learn that David was a great military leader, and an even better shepherd for God's chosen flock of sheep: You and I along-side Israel. Hallelujah.

Israel under Saul would be confronted by Edom and their men of valor, the race of giants. David was not the least intimidated. He had been anointed by the man of God, and he believed in the promises of God unconditionally. The God of David's ancestors had already given David victories over a bear and a lion when they attempted to steal his family sheep. David had incredible courage, and it came from believing the promises of God. He knew the Lord as shepherd over his life. He knew God was his armor and Jesus Christ as the Stone he would eventually wield to kill the Giant. The stone which the builders would eventually reject, is still protecting Israel and God's plan of redemption.

But first David had to face the Giant facing the people God anointed him to lead. King Saul had capitulated, and his faith was in the military might of Israel. Military might is good, when it is wielded for the purposes of God found in the Bible. An overreliance on Military might will be the downfall of America. Teshuva America! Repent and return to the God of King David. Place your total trust in him, and all of lives will be better for it.

David entered the Valley of Elah committed to providing his brothers with food and water and no doubt to provide a report to Jesse that his sons were ok. When he got there, he found the Edomites wielding an incredibly imposing figure in Goliath. His spear was the size of a weavers' beam. That is

The Valley of Elah

18 Feet in English. The Giant moved forward from Edomite lines to curse Israel and God. David was having none of this.

Saul reacted the way our Presidents do in national crisis, they threaten to wield our military might. The problem was the military lived in fear of retribution for worshipping the God of Abraham, Isaac, and Jacob. Our current situation in America. A soldier in America can no longer say: " For God and Country". He or she is forced to choose country and military might alone as God. We are living in our own Valley of Elah! Blasphemy.

Saul did what Narcissistic men in power do: They propose that we do what they would do. They offer their armor rather than the Armor of God. David tried Saul's plan. He tried on the Armor of Saul. Huge problem. David was a teenager who had not fully grown. Saul was 6'5". There was no way Saul's armor would have any effect when wielded by David.

Well, David did the courageous thing; He reminded Saul that God was able to provide all he needed to face his giant's. He reached down and picked up five smooth stones. Why five to face one Giant? Goliath had four brothers. He would face them all with the knowledge only of God's promise that he would one day occupy Saul's usurper throne. And that promise included that his offspring would bring forth God's eventual messiah. He could never do that if Goliath won. Well, David stuck with God's promises.

He walked calmly into the valley and called out the giant Goliath. He had underwear on and a sling. Goliath laughed. He did the one thing he could not afford to do with David and threw down his shield. He launched his spear which God blocked through angelic armor. Then he had only a single edge sword. Hallelujah. David had God's word alone and it is a two- edged sword. David loaded the sling with Jesus Christ as the stone which the builders would reject, and he launched the word of God straight into Goliath's forehead. Goliath fell, and David cut of his head with his own sword.

Then David sinned. He took the sword as a war trophy. That sword would surface later and cause David much hardship. Do not taunt the enemies of God. Kill them with the two-edged sword of the word of God. If it is God's will, they too will come over to God's side and live their life according to his promises.

Now what is the lesson from the valley of Elah? Too many to list all of them but I will take a stab at it. First, never doubt the promises of God contained in the two- edged sword of His word. Second, God's armor is all you ever need when you believe through faith that he is able to accomplish what he said in his word for your life. Third, a double minded man is unstable in all of his ways according to God. Saul went insane once he realized David had vanquished the Giant. David violated Israel's rules of War in never taking a spoil from uncircumcised Gentile nations. Today America and Israel are in treaties with nation's that God Hates! Our President had threatened to take spoil from our protracted enemy Iraq. This is a very dangerous statement. It quantifies that the reason the War in Iraq was fought was to secure oil.

The true Biblical reason the war has been waged is because God want's Israel and America to return to biblical thinking.

It is time for America to realize her God given destiny and move away from their march toward gentile pagan immorality. God want's the temple in Jerusalem to be built to receive Jesus Christ as Messiah. He wants his people Israel to recognize they dropped the ball in not recognizing Jesus Christ as Messiah. God accelerated his time clock in my lifetime. I am afraid America has relied on their military might and it needs to get back to reliance upon the armor of God; The Bible with its' two edges.

We are in our Valley of Elah Moment. Who will you choose to serve? As for me and my house, we will serve the Lord.

I existed in the Valley of Elah for a long time after returning from combat in Somalia. I prosecuted total war upon the enemies of America and I believe they are the enemies of God's plan for our lives. His plan is for all men to come to the knowledge of his messiah; Jesus Christ. Islam is the religion that will produce an Assyrian terrorist in the paradigm of Nimrod who will unite the world against the plan of God. It is a singular plan.

One day soon all of the false religions of the world, to include denominational Christianity ,will unite to stop Israel from finishing God's plan of redemption. A Satanic trinity is in the works as I pen these words.

The man of Lawlessness out of the Western leg of the revised Roman empire will soon be unveiled. He will unite with the

Pope in Rome as a false prophet and an Assyrian Muslim to form the Luciferian Trinity God warned us of. Where the carcasses lie, there the Eagles will gather.

It is the valley of Elah where they will muster their forces. Every nation with an Eagle as their symbol will unite to thwart the plan of God contained in the Word of God. To include America. It is an antisemitic plan which will see America persecute Jews and Christians worse than anyone in history. The plot has been hatched, the delusion of American church is fast fading. God is saving people in their homes without the need of three- dimensional spaces called church. Church long ago left God outside, and that is why he stands at the door and knocks: Because he is outside of our Christian churches.

The Church committed Heresy when it began to preach that God had replaced Israel. There is National Israel and saved Israel, known as the remnant to God. One day they will realize their mistake and cry out blessed is he who comes in the name of the Lord as they look upon him whom they have pierced. Hallelujah.

What do Christians do with this information. First open your Bible and find out if what I am Saying is true. Second, cry out to God for Mercy and Grace every Day. Third, pray for the peace of Jerusalem, for that peace is precluded by the return of Jesus Christ as Israel's messiah.

We live in a time the Bible has a lot to say about. Repent and return to solid Biblical instruction and pray for the salvation of your loved ones.

He was crucified upon a Cross of wood yet he created the hill upon which it stood!

Even so come Lord Jesus Christ.

RLTW John Burns 5-28-2020.

Can America Police Itself

According to God, all the thoughts of man are only evil continually. God alone has mercy and grace as His tenets for interaction with his creation. Men without God's plan, are simply not created to police themselves.

The purpose for sin in the world, is to teach us of our total dependence upon God for salvation from our sins. He created sin in us, to teach us the need to stay in covenant relationship with him. To be able to share God's attributes with a fallen world, humility must become the Christian call to repentance.

Salvation in Jesus Christ debt payment plan alone, that can lead men and society toward the possibility of once again, becoming Sons of God. Without salvation, society is inherently prejudice.

America has become the hub for exportation of all things Elohim abhors! Elohim is the first proper name in the Bible that rightly identifies God as creator of all things that exist. Both known and unknown. What we know about God, is that he is completely patient with us, the highest order in creation.

He has watched Adam and Eve Fail to only keep one commandment. He watched the descendants of Abraham exchange the worship of the Creator for worship of God's creation. He has watched Jews and Christians create a government of the people, for the people, and by the people, legislate him out of their lives. And we wonder why racism has become the chief mechanism by which Satan gets' Americans to question" Did God Say?".

Lucifer is the shining one of Ezekiel and Isaiah. He is the serpent in the garden whose oldest ploy is to get humans to question God's word and his plan of redemption. He has once again succeeded in getting Jews and Christians to focus on the flesh and not the spirit.

God birth's within every person born of a woman, who accepts the sacrifice God offered creation on Calvary, the gift of eternal life, regardless of skin color, or nationality, or political tribe. God is the God of creation, and he allowed us to kill him so he could raise creation from its' dead state. The reformation church that gave birth to American eugenic practices in churches across America, is in need of Jesus Christ resurrection. The Church is as guilty as the state for promoting racism in worship.

All White congregations, black liberation theology, Roman Catholic antisemitism. God hates all of these practices. God is a HUMAN racist. He loves the sinner, and yet he abhors sin. He does not judge by outward appearance, but by the content of your character. Only people bent on the demise of God's plan of redemption, purvey in racism.

I wonder when the last time American preachers addressed God's perfect will in all issues that relate to race. I know that we all have common ancestors. That is why God goes out of his way to include genealogies in the bible. We are all descended from Noah and his wife, then back to Adam and Eve the mother, and father of all living.

Did you know that Noah 's wife had three sons? Did you know that one was black, one was white, and one was Asian? Probably not. The American Christian church long ago married the world system. This world system follows a eugenic program. And no- where is it worse than in America.

How did Noah's sons make it on that boat for so many days, weeks, and months? Their father was led by God's Holy Spirit and God's revealed word was Noah's guide for raising three sons who all looked different. The Bible is the only book that will return America to sanity when it comes to human interaction. I refuse to believe we are different. God created us in his triune image. We all have sinned and fall short of the glory of God, and are in need of God's extreme measure by which he is redeeming his entire creation.

American politicians hijack the narrative each time easy lies replace hard truth. Humans are inherently flawed from birth. We all share the trait of original sin. We all have the choice to accept that God equally died for each person born of a woman. To purvey in race, is to deny God is the way, the truth, and the life.

There is a foundational reason why America is completely and inherently racist. The foundation our government has advanced, completely confuses our children on all issues dealing with morality. The Church in America with all of its' forms and fashions is to blame.

Silent pulpits since 1963. When one political party decided to legislate God out of the lives of our children in their advance and march toward Darwinian evolution as the moral compass for our country. It begins in public school when you register your child for pre-k. The indoctrination they hope for begins in earnest in children as young as four.

The Bible being taken out of our children's lives has hurt us a nation more than any other political decision in history. If our country is ever to return to greatness, then the moral foundations found in the Bible must be made available to our children in public education once again.

God has always provided his creation with their own ability to believe or not believe in His bible plan. For the government to deny that right, is exactly why we are still debating race in America, and how we interact with each other daily. I personally take the high road. I take people one at a time. Judging only by the content of their character and not by the color of a persons' skin. We all become a little more ignorant when we purvey in debates about race. The very definition of ignorance is to condemn something before investigating. Just maybe we would be a lot better off if we spent more time with those who do not look like us.

I have found in this life that I have learned how to resist all pre-suppositions about race by spending time with people of color. My entire life testifies that I have gone out of my way to remain open to all things human. My life has been incredible and I have learned that most of our stereotypes advanced by news organizations, government in any form, and public educators, do not actually fit our American experience.

There are plenty of injustices in this life that God alone can make right through Jesus Christ death, burial and resurrection alone. Any action to correct social wrongs will never be possible if we depend on government to find the answers. They created our problems. Asking the coyote to fix the hen house is insanity!

Teshuva is America's only hope at racial reconciliation. A return to sound Biblical morality gleaned from both Testaments of our Bible, is our only hope and it must be offered to our children in public education as an elective. No community has been hurt more by removing the Bible from public school than the black community in America.

Martin Luther King Jr. preached salvation from the Old Testament. He understood all persons need for mercy and grace. He had been to the mountaintop and visited with Moses. They both have a destiny that will see them reach the promised land.

The very administration that was pretending to advance civil rights wanted Martin Luther King Jr. silenced for preaching morality from the Hebrew bible. The morality the Kennedy administration revolved around is based upon chaos, and political elite persons ruling the poor class in America. Removing the bible and prayer from our children's lives advanced that morality.

Today they control every aspect of the message they want us to hear. They have enslaved us to their plan for saving us. If America is to ever be great again, a war to place God back in our children's' lives' is the only way forward. America is craving a king David to put God back in the lives of our kids! Hallelujah.

In reviewing the recent killing of a black man, I had to confront what I already knew would happen. The charlatan black men who hijacked the black community after Martin Luther King's death, would end up front and center fleecing the black community in America. Dr. King's death gave birth to a new theology in America that is counterintuitive to the bible and its' message, and it was hijacked by men who claim to preach God's will for our lives. It is called black liberation theology. It is racist.

A house divided against itself can never stand. Unless the black community returns to sound bible teaching, the eugenic minded black leaders who have signed off on the systematic murder of 41 million black babies in the wombs of black mothers will succeed at destroying your incredibly vibrant communities. They are in bed with the true white racists in America, the national Democratic party.

The Black Community in America must demand the Bible be made available again to their children. They must demand accountability of their current President for his role in drafting the 1994 crime bill, which has destroyed three to four generations of black families with incarceration levels that have no end in sight. At the heart is a eugenic mind that permeates the political elite class of people who believe they are the chosen stock to rule and reign over us. They are black, white, Asian, and Latino, and they do not support bible morality!

America needs to wake up from 70 years of Democratic and Republican fleecing. Somehow in the middle of all their race baiting, common people have found ways to overcome racism without their help. That is what scares the race baiters the most. They can- not have us moving away from dependence upon government if their advance toward ruling us eternally is to succeed.

Jews and Christians who love God must unite and place God back in the lives of our children. They have much to lose. They purvey in everything that divides us, and they are unable as a mechanism to fix the foundations that they have dug up and thrown away.

What would scare both Parties into uniting is the shot of a third party succeeding in America that has God's morality as their platform. The bible being there only book by which to advance morality. Imagine a leader who purveys in hard truth and can- not be bought with easy lies. A man willing to die for the testimony of Jesus Christ found in the Old Testament. The Old Testament preaching model worked for Jesus Christ and it worked For Martin Luther King Jr.

What I know about my God is that he is faithful to those who promote his plan for humanity and all else is human vanity. I will meet Dr. King in heaven and thank him for planting a seed that led to me confronting racism that permeated my entire existence. I was inherently not, a bad person, I had been taught eugenics since my first day in kindergarten. I was my mom and dad's Man. I was special, and my segregated school was on full display.

God had an amazing sense of humor in my life. He opened my eyes to the deception of the two- party system in America that is not designed to ever wash its' citizens feet. It is based upon voters giving away their rights from God, in favor of having rights legislated by congress. That congress should never have the right to legislate the God of the bible in any way. Our rights as Americans come from the creator who permeates the pages of our most holy bible.

Racism in this world will only ever be overcome when Jesus Christ returns to set up a government where Elohim is alone worshipped. Every polytheistic belief system in the world is inherently racist. America has become the purveyor of polytheism while pretending to separate church in any form from the state apparatus.

Politicians routinely hijack God's word in times of crisis. They quote God when it is convenient to enflame their base of voters. God is not amused by your ruse of outward piety. He is judging his creation based upon his word and their inward conviction of it. Hallelujah.

He was crucified upon a cross of wood, yet he created the hill upon which it stood.

Even so come Lord Jesus Christ.

RLTW John Burns 7-28-2021.

PTSD Answer

I first began to hear the term PTSD growing up in a home, where both of my grandfather's fought in World War 2, and I came from a family that had a rich 20th century history of serving in the United States military. My exposure to someone suffering from the diagnosis would not occur until I served in the United States Army in the 75th Ranger Regiment.

My beloved third bn of the 75th Ranger Regiment has distinguished itself with a rich history of providing heroes to America. When I served in the 1990's we would hold an annual Ranger rendezvous and never was one better than the rendezvous of 1992. It would see the beginning of bond's being formed between Rangers of all modern American conflicts from World War 2 to the modern Regiments participation in Operation Just Cause, the invasion of the Republic of Panama in 1989.

It was not Viet Nam, but at the time, it was all third bn. had as a modern combat heritage. None the-less, in 1992 I would meet men who were true American heroes.

PTSD Answer

From Bull Dawson, the Lieutenant who led the Rangers onto the beaches of Normandy. To Ranger Phil Piazza a Ranger World War Two legend.

The Korean War would see the Heroic African- American Ranger company that jumped into Munsan-Ni in 1951. I would have the pleasure of meeting many of these trail blazers.

Viet Nam would produce the first Rangers who would fight a very unpopular war, but it would produce many American heroes.

Dave Dolby would receive the Medal of Honor from Lyndon Johnson and do four more tours post award. That is what defines my America. All of these men had been exposed to the horrors of war. Yet, they came home to an America where they did not necessarily agree with their countrymen at home, yet they still went to Viet Nam. Most Rangers multiple times.

How did their experience affect them when they got home?

I now have Ranger brothers with multiple tours, some with 15 combat deployments, hindsight is 20/20. I now have the experience of leaving the military after ground combat, and I am finally qualified to speak on the issue.

Personally, after two days of not being in the Army I realized I was completely different than anyone I shared space with. The first people to suffer were my ex -wife and daughter. I did not realize that everyone did not dance with the devil behind the gunsights of an M16 rifle! My world would never be the same.

I first realized most Americans take the price of all their Bill of Rights freedoms for granted when I encountered Vietnam veterans at Fort Benning. These great Americans served in the most thankless war to date. And America greeted them with violent protests.

Then right in the middle of Vietnam, America realized it had abolished slavery, but did very little to improve the lives of African-Americans. Even as they broke down racial barriers in military service, their lives at home had changed very little in America. Couple that with the fact that America had begun fighting a war in an Opium producing country and it made it home with our soldiers as they survived warfare, only to succumb to addiction and suicide.

After World War 1 a total prohibition on alcohol saved countless American lives as soldiers returned from the trenches with shell shock.

World War 2 would see many men return to America and drown themselves in Alcohol. By 1992 the stories I heard about men who served in many European battles coming home to die a pauper's death as an alcoholic, frightened me. When I left the military some-how I lost the taste for constant alcohol. Thank God.

But I had physical injuries, while suppressing the thoughts about men who were my brothers on Earth that had fallen, and now I would not grow old with them telling stories of our experiences in combat and peace,

I developed an unhealthy liking for anything Narcotic. If it could make me not think about my lost forever friends, I took it...It developed what the Bible refers to as a Stronghold. Interesting that the original Greek word used in scripture to describe strongholds is the Greek word PHARMAKIA. From where we get pharmaceutical.

American politicians cannot continue to place the burden of military service in war upon Americans, while they themselves are writing laws that contradict why they fight. Soldiers volunteer to defend the constitution against all enemies foreign and domestic.

The Bill of Rights defines who their enemy is on their private property. The Constitution left it open about who Is an American.

The national myth that America was founded by 57 white guys in Philadelphia, rewrites 160 years of well- established truth. Puritans and Jewish sailors founded Plymouth Rock and signed the first document governing their behavior in the new world.

The Mayflower Compact stated that our laws would be derived from the Bible and the God of Abraham, Isaac, Jacob, and Joseph. While New Testament tenets taught by Jesus Christ would govern individual conduct of the Pilgrims. How we got to 1787 must be taught to our children so that America's foundation does not become our Achilles heel.

96-99 million red Indians died to give us slavery and an imperfect beginning.

The Civil War proved that we could murder each other. Lincoln taught us God's way was perfect. FDR, while leading us out of the great depression, and through the Majority of WW2, also packed the Supreme court with judges who for the first time began to legislate rather than interpret established law.

Rowe V. Wade is the fruit of FDR's seedtime. Morality must never be legislated by government, unless that Government defines who our creator as individuals is!

The First Amendment guaranteed a Christian man had no redress of grievances, for the second amendment is the only means by which an American citizen can guarantee his or her God, is the God worshipped on his or her private property. For the weapons a Christian fight's with, are spiritual not carnal, for the pulling down of strongholds.

Separation of church and state was made real on Calvary. The government in any form will never legislate in favor of our creators' plan. Jesus Christ died fighting the religious leaders and the Roman government officials. American soldiers are asked to leave their homes and neighborhoods. Most all white, all black, or in some-way segregated neighborhoods to join an American military controlled by a congress and President that most times could never empathize with their plight. Soldiers rarely come from elitist backgrounds.

They fight for causes they would never vote for. Their pay never matches their commitment. Coming home will never match their time serving in uniform. The bonds formed with men they probably thought they did not like before War, can never be breached. Loyalty has forged these iron relationships. Now it is time for that service to be more then recognized.

The Veterans Administration is failed socialized medicine! Social programs in America need to return some sanity to our system. If everyone is on disability for PTSD, then America suffers as a country. Our national debt is unsustainable. The workforce that built our post world- war 2 world is a thing of the past.

Veterans deserve the best Doctors and best care in the world. If that were available upon leaving the service, less American veterans will suffer debilitating PTSD.

Waiting for VA programs is causing irrational decisions by veterans to self- medicate. The scars of War do not recede. Time heals all wounds, and makes mental stressors easier to control when we acknowledge the past experiences of Vietnam vets in discharging this generation from post war service.

We recruit men and women from our communities where upward mobility is almost nonexistent. They serve honorably and heroically. They return to their communities and jobs are nonexistent. Narcotics are everywhere. Combat is non explainable!!!

Men can tell noble stories and people may stand in awe. In the end men die. Some very well trained, and some with very little training, they still die. Asking our young vulnerable poor to return to substandard care and a Congress unwilling to do anything but disagree and race bait, and they are left with their hands over their face and their heart embarrassed to admit they served.

This country is imperfect. It will not get any better erasing our well-established history. What can we learn from if not our mistakes? I have been home from combat in Somalia for twenty- eight - years now. I am watching some of the bravest men I have ever met, struggle with their past, and especially their losses. I defer to my creator, whom I call Jesus Christ to fix my software problems.

When I bought a Ford, I expected Henry Ford to warranty my purchase.

God warrantied his purchase when he allowed himself to be nailed to a cross to pay our sin debt.

I have been to 45 countries on 5 continents. I love America and I love Americans the most. Our ability to compromise is our greatest strength. How-ever, to compromise with an American system that overpromises, is not in my soldier heart.

I pray for my country to experience God's awakening revival. My Soldier friends need to look to the creator of the universe to heal their software. It begins by acknowledging you are in need of Justification. Justification comes with your personal belief in the death, burial, and resurrection of Jesus Christ.

The American church experience unfortunately most often ends there. Get in the Bible and find out what God says about your future with him on earth and in future heaven. Now, have the humility to admit that it is ok to have feelings of guilt.

War takes the best Americans. I pray that they were free of the guilt that comes through wartime actions. God does not love war. It is not his perfect will! However, his permissive will allows men to murder each other for other than Godly purposes. You are not alone. God anticipated that, and left us with his Holy Spirit to comfort, correct, and guide us down the narrow path that leads to salvation.

No greater Love hath a man than this, that he lay down his life for his friends.

Jesus Christ led the Way. He laid down his life for you, for you to spend eternity with him.

PTSD robs men of their connection to a loving creator. They feel judgement and guilt. The Church is failing these men. They do not need another church; they need the connection to their creator. The message of Mercy must again resonate so Grace can appear in soldier's lives. Empathy is our watchword.

Ask a soldier or veteran to tell you about themselves. Without any presuppositions. They are each different but all very much loved. The stigma attached to this problem has to reach past the disability rating. Money will never fix a soldier's wounded heart. Understanding without condemnation will lead us all away from ignorance.

I live each and every day with the knowledge that I came home and my brothers did not. Now I must live for us both, and in my case now too many brothers to count. I just put my head down, my hands to the plow, and harvest the fruit of repentance with God's justification as my reward. My heart is sanctified to the will of God my savior. As a veteran you are loved by your mates. We are all coming home every day.

Begin a relationship with Jesus Christ today and symptoms of despair retreat. Hope will be restored.

Vietnam vets taught me there will always be a percentage of our American population without the will to stomach or accept your sacrifice. That is quite alright. They cannot stomach that God loves them either. That is the real shame.

You represented America with courage and conviction. How much courage does it take to have everything paid for by someone else? This is their dilemma! Jesus Christ paid my sin debt and I paid for their freedom, with my blood in Somalia, only to have American liberals, deny his sacrifice on the cross.

I want to spend eternity in heaven with American veterans.

Your time on earth determines heavenly rewards, and your inheritance of eternal life can only come through surrender to God's one plan for your life.

PTSD is not God's plan.

The diagnosis from the Veterans Administration may seem good today, as it brings' monetary reward. Does everyone who served in a combat Zone deserve 100% of their life to be managed by a failed system of medical socialism?

The Rating Board will happily give you 100% if you are willing to be controlled by them. This is the first step to taking away your rights under our Constitution and Bill of Rights.

Democrats live under the yoke of bondage to lawlessness. The political elite class of politicians, who after Vietnam began to lobby congress for better treatment of veterans as they returned from a very unpopular war that they profited from for 16 years.

Arriving at the Conclusion that anyone who deployed to Vietnam must be traumatized when in reality only one percent of those who serve in a combat zone are involved in two- way gunfights.

It is a Lie to claim PTSD to inconvenience taxpayers to fund your mental instability if you have never fired a shot in anger.

You have convinced yourself that you are owed what men who now have 18 years in actual combat deserve. What they earned.

You are no different than someone who believes they are entitled to money from our government because of poverty.

If a Man does not work, he should not eat!

Any veteran who lies to secure monetary benefit from a government only interested in taking away their 1st and 2d amendment rights, deserves nothing from our treasury.

I fell prey to the narrative that anyone who could prove he served in a Ranger unit during Vietnam deserves 100% disability rating. Most of those men who never were in a two-way gunfight, live in a vacuum of Lies.

The Truth only comes in one color and true service is when you expect nothing from a government that exists only to create chaos.

War is necessary to secure the freedoms described in the Constitution. America never takes a spoil, just like ancient Israel.

If you are a Warrior who served to defend our way of life, get home, go to college, and actually help America by getting a job and start an American family.

It is actually unpatriotic to collect 100% if you have never killed for the United States way of life. If you are collecting 100% because you are weak, then Ranger up! America is not going to survive this entitlement mentality for soon we will be forced to once again defeat enemies here at home who threaten our great system through programs that are draining our bank.

If you are draining the bank do not think I am your friend.

There are two types of Americans: Those willing to defend our way of life and those who just live here! Which one are you?

Service must never contain monetary incentive. If you reach 20 years of service then you deserve everything from the

American treasury. I too fell prey to the PTSD narrative. Free money, hell yeah!

Then my friends began coming home with 26 years in service and 18 deployments with thousands of gun-fight's and I do not deserve what these men deserve from the American Treasury.

The Veterans' Administration has become a slush fund for all kinds of lawlessness. Paying men to not work is ungodly. Teach a man to plow a field and he can feed a generation. Train him to accept American scraps and he can barely feed himself.

Leadership requires that I speak the truth and it only comes in one color. Our American monetary system has been under attack by forces bent on destroying America through apathy. If you are so selfish that you believe the Americans you claim to have defended really deserve to go bankrupt for your supposed service then we deserve the coming internal civil war.

Time to reset our government just like the Declaration of Independence requires citizens do. The Culture War that removed the Bible from public school is now reaping the rewards of Socialism.

Sending men who feel entitled, to secure our way of life, ensures our way of life will be over very soon.

There is one- way home to Beulah. This is not our home. We exist in a temporary tabernacle called the body, but your spirit and soul go on forever. The belief in the shed blood of the lamb: Jesus Christ, guarantees eternal life with our creator.

We are at war here at home against the forces of darkness who have guaranteed the abandonment wrath of God is manifest.

They will do everything to regain power and keep you in monetary bondage to scraps which will soon disappear. They hate warriors even more then they hate war. I am an American warrior from the mold of Robert Rogers and Francis Marion.

Patriotism continues in your life when you choose to serve Jesus Christ. Return from war and be productive, especially if you feel you are entitled to anything but what they promised at your enlistment.

Men who have actually served in war may pretend to respect you, however, getting a job ensures you will return to productivity after warfare.

Men have died for you to have the ability to feel sorry for yourself. If you truly respect those men you served with, honor them by becoming productive Americans.

It begins by allowing Jesus Christ to change your software from inside out. lose all pre-suppositions about religion and read the Bible from cover to cover and study to show yourself approved.

Choose this day whom you will serve, as for me and my house we will serve the Lord! John Burns, Panama, and Somalia Veteran.

Even so come Lord Jesus Christ. 7-29-2021 He was crucified upon a cross of wood, yet he created the hill upon which it stood.

Parenting Perversion

This is the hardest truth I have ever confronted in my life. I am the victim of an upbringing that looked great on the surface, but from a Bible perspective, I am a victim of Satan's deception. I forgive the people involved, and pray for their salvation alone in the blood of Jesus Christ.

God instructed Adam and Eve to realize there was one reason why a man should leave his mother and father, and cleave unto the bosom of his wife. Malachi 3 is the key to understanding the singular reason God instituted the marriage covenant on earth. God was seeking a Godly seed.

Pro-creation is when a man and woman are equal in pro-genitorship, and for the purpose of teaching your child God's singular plan of redemption. Have you left your mother and father or are you still clinging to your mother's bosom in all matter's concerning your marriage? Do your children see you glorifying their mother?

God does not require a man to leave his mother and father until he is ready to be Biblically responsible for a woman. The Hebrew mind reminds us that most men are not ready for marriage until about 30 years of Age. Levirite marriage is one of total responsibility for the bride to be. The father of the groom must petition the would- be bride's father, and he must first pay the dowry to show that the man's father is behind their son, and they will honor the commitment to provide for the bride for life financially.

The covenant is initiated when the father of the groom finds a potential bride for their son. The father then approaches the bride to be's father with the proposal. Upon acceptance of the offer, the groom to be, has the father initiate a financial dowry to prove it is now a lifetime commitment. The groom returns to his father's house, and begins to build a room addition onto his father's house and he patiently awaits the marriage. The bride is veiled, as proof that she is committed and she will accept the marriage proposal. She awaits word that her home is prepared and the date is set for her to be married.

In my life, none of these Biblical requirements were initiated by my father. I have yet to meet a Christian who has? The reason for this is that every religion practiced in America is antisemitic, and Eugenic in nature. America has gone the way of Baalim.

While pretending to know the God of the Bible, Americans cling to Roman church tradition. Martin Luther's Reformation failed miserably to reform the Church into an Acts of the Apostles church. While understanding Faith alone through Grace can save a sinner, Luther was devoutly antisemitic and did not return to teaching mercy and grace from an Old Testament perspective.

He allegorized scripture, and failed to recognize the kingdom from God's perspective as outlined in the Old Testament. Jesus Christ every word in the New Testament is a repeat of his words from the Old Testament. He is the God who keeps his promises for eternity and he has not changed.

He has never replaced Israel or his requirement to stay married for life. Train up a child in the way they should go and when they are old, they will not depart from it. My Father divorced my mother, and I divorced my first wife. Blasphemy.

The Marriage covenant is a mirror image and paradigm for teaching us the eternal covenant Jesus Christ entered into on the Cross of Calvary. God entered our dimension of time to enter into a marriage covenant with anyone who will believe in his death to pay their sin debt. The resurrection of Christ should revive your dead thinking about marriage, and its' single purpose in God's eyes.

The single purpose for getting married is to provide God with offspring that love and believe in his plan of redemption. That plan is also singular. God became a man in the womb of a virgin Jewish girl to be born king of the Jews. That is Jesus Christ inheritance from the Father. He will one day receive the Kingdom of David in Jerusalem. That event occurs after the final seven years of gentile reign on Earth.

Jesus Christ is returning to judge all of the kingdoms of the earth. But not before he receives his reward for dying for all sinners from all eternity. His reward is a Gentile and Jewish bride of believers in his debt payment plan. He died to pay the only debt that matters when we die: Our sin debt to God the Father. Hallelujah.

The koinonos of God, which gentile believers refer to as the church, are Jesus Christs' bride. His death, burial, and resurrection were rewarded by God the Father, by providing the Holy Spirit to find Jesus a suitable bride. He is the bridegroom of creation. His bride is anyone who answers the still soft voice of God when he says I stand at the door and knock. If any man hears my voice, I will come in and sup with him. That is God's Marriage proposal for his son.

It is God the Holy Spirit who asks for our hand in marriage. It is eternal, and when you say I believe, he will never leave you, nor forsake you. He will provide all of your needs according to his riches in glory. Marriage is eternal in God's kingdom. Will you accept the dowry Jesus Christ paid on Calvary to have God betroth you to Christ for all eternity?

When Jesus Christ ascended to heaven after the resurrection, he returned to the father's house to build us a mansion. The pattern is continued from Genesis 2. Instead of building a room onto the Father's house, Jesus Christ is building every believer a mansion to spend eternity with Christ. This proves the exalted position of the bride of Christ. It is a subset of the body of Christ. The body of Christ has a future, different from the bride of Christ.

The Bride of Christ are those believers who are willing to die for Jesus, and that belief leads to missionary outreach with all of your endeavors. The command to go ye into all the world and preach the gospel, is for every believer.

If you are dependent on Church tradition for your salvation, you are probably not the bride of Christ. You may be a member of the body of Christ, but you will not be going to the marriage supper in heaven at the rapture. You will go through the tribulation, and your only hope then is martyrdom.

God reminds believers that divorce is only acceptable if the bride has committed adultery. Every church in America commits adultery every Sunday when they worship on a day other than God's established sabbath. It is Friday evening through Saturday evening. It happens to be one of the two days Jesus Christ will be in the millennial temple during the millenial Reign. The other day is the new moon.

God is on a lunar cycle in keeping time, while Church commits adultery by serving Rome on a solar cycle. There are 360 day years in the bible year, yet, professing Christian's practice synecretism, and meld Roman pagan beliefs with a little bit of earthly Jesus.

Every holiday venerated by Christian churches in America, are adulterous at best, and, completely pagan in practice. Christmas, New Years, Valentines' Day, Easter, Birthdays, Mother's Day, Father's Day, Funerals, and yes weddings, are all pagan fertility practices and they got their foundations in Babylon.

God is on a Jewish liturgical schedule and it will continue on into eternity. He does not play let's make a deal. He gave us the Word of God and said this is the deal. Jesus Christ worshipped on Gods' schedule when he walked the earth, and he will worship on Gods' schedule in the millennium when he and I receive his kingdom. Hallelujah.

Divorce was something that my father alone practiced. Every brother of his who married, stayed married for life. His parents stayed married for life. What happened in my dads' life to make him leave my mother?

My Dad is a practicing Roman Catholic. Their mother church model deifies women. While pretending to be externally pious, Roman Catholics do not believe in the trinity for salvation. They do not understand God's total will for their lives, and they more than any other Religion, do what is right in their own eyes. If they would return to individual Bible literacy, many more believers in God would stay married.

Protestants are much worse. They have divided Gods' kingdom into 29 Denominations in America, and divorce amongst Christians is higher than among non- Christians. Why should young people want to get married? God has turned America over to a reprobate mind. They cannot discern right from wrong, and doing what feels good to them, is what they think is best for their own selfish thinking.

Divorce is now the norm in church and synagogue! Blasphemy. America is under the abandonment wrath of God. They subscribe to government morality. Homosexuality, Transgenderism, Adultery. All have become main stream behavior in America and it permeates Church. Gay Bishops and pastors with Jesus Christ on their church titles? Churches have compromised and there is a price that is going to be paid!

God loves the homosexual. God Loves the transgender person. He Loves the adulterer. He cannot however exist in the presence of sin. We must all pray for America. Do not blame these people for their infidelity, and alternate morality. Blame your church, and their failed leadership model, for those are whom God will hold accountable.

Jesus Christ died for all sinners. He was raised to life to raise you to life from dead thinking about marriage and alternate moral conviction. Teshuva! Repent and return to God and his Bible for questions about marriage and morality. We are in the final phase of Gods' Grace, and soon the world will be existing without true believers, for they will be gone in the upcoming Rapture.

The purpose of the rapture is for God to redeem the creation and to chasten the Jewish remnant for the last time. He will judge every gentile kingdom and they will perish. None more harshly than America. The Church in America married the government. They compromise in the voting booth, and professing Christians actually vote for people who support and practice abortion.

Providing God with Biblically raised children is the purpose of marriage. To murder children in the womb, denies that fetus of the right to choose Jesus Christ.

You are supporting murder, and God is watching you in that voting booth. Every one of those fetuses will receive a glorified body. They are currently in the bosom of Abraham awaiting the rapture of the church. They will rise with believers who chose to marry Jesus Christ in this life. Are you married to

Jesus Christ or are you ok with pretending to love him for two hours a week on Sunday? Get back in the Bible, and see if what John Burns is saying is true. Your life will never be the same.

The 1960's changed everything in my America. God was legislated out of my life. The Bible was outlawed in my education experience and I dropped out of high school. My parents never mentioned the word of God. Catholic priests taught me to self- indulge my passions. I believe they all are homosexual because there is a homosexual nightclub on the Vatican premises specifically for priests, deacons, and bishops.

Nuns are temple prostitutes. They place themselves under Satanic bondage by denying God access to their wombs through his covenant of marriage. Their leanings toward virginity and outward piety are absolute sin. I am praying for you all to escape bondage. God needs you to raise children devoted to the God of the Bible. Leave the Babylonian mystical Roman Catholic church and join the kingdom of God.

Get married and have Godly offspring. That is what truly pleases God.

I have children by two different women. One I actually married and divorced, and one I actually looked at as my reward for being born. My thinking was perverse at best. It was definitely sinful and requires repentance and forgiveness. To repent means to move away from the sin needing salvation. I have remarried 20 years ago. I have remained faithful to God and I intend to stay married for life. I am practicing my faith so that my children may learn from my fidelity.

I pray God has mercy on my children and they receive the grace of God. I pray for my sons' salvation and I pray for a long marriage to his wife. I am praying for my daughter to receive Jesus Christ. I pray she will learn from me that she is a child of God with a biblical future.

Human sexuality was created for use in the marriage covenant only. Any sex outside of marriage is sin, and requires repentance and return to biblical literacy found only in the Bible. If you are living in sexual perversion, you probably have never learned God's way from the Bible.

No church or parent has ever taught me sexuality from a Godly perspective. I doubt many Americans have heard what I am teaching either. America must return to the bible with both testaments being taught. God has never changed. He still feels the same way about marriage.

Repentance leads to the love and grace of God. Sexual perversion has decimated America. Our government hates the God of the Bible. They will never wash your feet like Jesus Christ continues to do. I have never witnessed foot washing in any of the 24 Denominations of church I have visited. I have experienced foot washing by Christians in prison ministry. Inmates know why they are in prison, I have yet to meet a modern Christian who is in church for reasons they actually understand.

Pastors refuse to preach and teach God's version of marriage. I truly believe it is not profitable. Most would have to confront their own thinking about marriage. Jesus Christ died to raise dead men to life. Pastors today are in need of Godly biblical revelation. Return to God's marriage covenant.

I Love my father, and my mother. I Love my siblings my father and step mother gave me in this life. I do not support their ideas about marriage and human sexuality for it violates God's moral compass direction which is the only true north when dealing with sex and marriage.

I pray for my Family to receive biblical salvation in Christ alone. He loves you and he is asking for your hand in marriage.

He was crucified upon a Cross of wood Yet he created the hill upon which it stood!

Even so come Lord Jesus Christ.

RLTW John Burns 5-28-2020.

Deification of the Woman

The two-party system in America is completely corrupt. I believe at the heart of the problem is the move away from legislating for the morality God alone gave us in the Bible, toward the Greek eugenic model practiced by both parties since our founding. Greek thinking is exactly what is wrong with America.

The Greeks were Polytheists. Their pantheon was a solar centric pantheon where the sun was the center of their universe. The Egyptians of antiquity had a solar centric pantheon. The Greeks eventually took over Egypt and married their mythology to the Egyptian mythology to give us synecretism. It is defined as the mixing of two or more modes of thinking about life and death.

Synecretism occurs when a person born of a woman, mixes the worship of the creator, with the religious practices of worshipping everything God created. The Hebrew Bible is the only book where we can glean the foundational truth as to when people first exchanged God as creator, with worship of His creation.

After experiencing every polytheistic religion on my travel as an Airborne Ranger in the United States military, I have come to some hard truths about my United States of America. When America today speaks of God, it is in the context of Synecretism. Our government has actually legislated God out of our lives and we have willingly stood by as they exchanged our God for their fertility religion.

It begins early in the life of our children. Now America is under the abandonment wrath of God, and we have one last chance to get back in favor with our creator. It has nothing to do with sin. It has to do with how you believe all sin is paid for in God the creator's economy.

According to the Hebrew bible which Jesus Christ preached from, God created four things. The Hebrew word create is the word Bara. From nothing, something!

God's creative name is ELOHIM. Every Hebrew word can be gleaned from three Hebrew characters found in every Hebrew word. Using Hebrew hermeneutics and the law of First mention, God is always ELOHIM. His creative name is gleaned from the Hebrew characters Aleph, Lamed, He, Yod, Mem.

The Aleph is representative of an Ox. It is both a beast of burden and an animal to be sacrificed. The Lamed is the shepherds crook or staff. It has two ends which represent God's divine attributes of mercy and grace. The He is representative of the very breath of God. It is the Spirit of God. It is pronounced as RUAH. It represents how God is present with every believer in his plan of redemption. The Spirit alone orders a righteous man's footsteps. The Yod is representative of the open hand. God the creator has given us the open hand of blessing, and, the open hand of correction. It chastens us through study of the Hebrew bible.

To ask God to bless you, willingness to be chastened by God is at the heart of our American problem when it comes to understanding the mind of God our creator. The Yod is the place from where God doles out mercy and grace. To receive the open hand of God, a believer must make Yeshua the Lord of his or her life.

The fear of the Lord is the beginning of wisdom. To become wise, one must first believe in God and his preposterous debt payment plan. Then God will return the open hand of blessing upon America. The Mem is representative of the living water. It is the living water through whom God measures mercy and grace in the life of the believer. The Palm of his righteous right hand, is the place where God hold's believers. The palm is also where God holds' the entire created Universe. The living water is yeshua ha messiah, Jesus the Christ.

The biggest insult a person born of a woman, heaps on God, is to deny him as creator. We are without excuse. One day, it is the palm of God's hand that will roll up our universe. It is with the palm of his hand that he will defeat the nations of the earth who have worked to get him out of the lives of our children. It is with the palm of the hand that parents chasten children, and it is indicative of God to do the same with his creation. If you wonder why our children are confused, it is because you did not incorporate the palm of your hand in their education experience.

Back to the creation. Elohim created the heavens and the earth. He created man. And he created angels. He did not create woman. Eve is the mother of all living after she was taken from Adam who God created, and she was made the glory of the man. Eve became equal to Adam only in progenitor-ship. It takes two to make the pattern complete. One man with one woman producing Godly offspring.

America insults God every time we push to legislate equality between man and woman. Every time we push the narrative that it is a woman's right alone to choose to murder their offspring, it denies God as creator with complete sovereignty over the womb. It denies Adam was created in God's image. It attacks the Hebrew bible narrative that God alone can control reproduction.

It is refreshing to me to see so many forced sterilizations by planned parenthood, making the news. It still occurs in America on every Indian reservation. Indian women are sterilized without ever having a choice. And every time an Indian woman enters the health clinic started by the Eugenic minded Democrats who have murdered them for convenience, that beautiful Indian woman is sterilized.

They have convinced former Christian people in black communities that it was convenient to kill your offspring rather than further burden society with the possibility that they may drain our government coffers on social programs. Imagine if the black community had the FORTY -Three Million black babies the Democrats killed, to vote in elections. Imagine how many more Clarence Thomas's, and

Deification of the Woman

Ben Carson's America would have to serve us in this time of moral crisis. If we had just one more Candace Owens raised by one more moral Grandfather, America would indeed be great!

The Deification of women in America did not start in America. It started with the first rebellion orchestrated by Nimrod at Babel. It was at Babel that the world was divided into creation and creator worshippers.

Those that rebelled, began to worship and deify everything Elohim created. Nimrod became Pontifex Maximus. He named himself a god. His wife Semiramis became the wife of God and the mother to the son of God. His name was Tammuz 1.

I firmly believe Nimrod was under the influence of the Nephillim who were the offspring of angels and the daughters of men. I believe Semiramis had an adulterous affair with a fallen angel and had Tammuz. He had the DNA of the Woman and the DNA of a fallen male angel. From this pantheon come the Greek and Roman mythologies that permeate American society.

The Greeks are the society that gave us the well born stock. Our entire Government model and education model comes from the Greek and Roman mind. Elohim has an eastern Hebrew mind and his word is his promise to the creation.

Hebrew alone is the language of God's love. God separated East and West in Jerusalem. He is again unifying the world he created, and Hebrew is being spoken in Israel.

To understand the power behind the deification of women in America, one must lose all pre-suppositions about everything feminine and everything you believe. You must submit to the teaching's found only in the Old Testament of our Hebrew Bible.

The foundation for all pagan belief systems emanated from heaven after Lucifer's rebellion. He alone led one third of the angels to rebel against God. They were cast to the Earth after the creation. God expelled Lucifer and one-third of the Angels from Heaven. He gave Lucifer control of the earth which led to God creating Adam.

On day one God began reducing entropy. It involves moving from chaos to order. God created the heavens and the earth perfect, Lucifer rebelled, God flooded the earth the first time, then took to restoring order in His creation. First order of business was to create it inhabitable for a replacement for Lucifer.

God must be worshipped, and heaven lost its' worship leader when Lucifer rebelled. Adam was meant to be the replacement of Lucifer.

God created the earth uniquely for human habitation: He instituted physics, chemistry, mathematics, and literature. All to prepare to welcome Adam's suitable helpmeet. But not before Adam understood reproduction. It was designed only to be practiced between male and female species and only with their own genetic kind. Animals are never homosexual. Only human's defy God and engage in Immoral sexual relationships.

Deification of the Woman

Most animals stay with one mate for life. Human's divorce and remarry for sport. Then humans expect to have God save them. American men divorce because our society deifies women. First, by putting un-do pressure on our daughters to always be pretty on the outside, while neglecting God on the inside.

The oversexualization of our sons and daughters has led to the abandonment wrath of God. America is at the crossroads. Will we continue down the path of complete immorality or choose to repent and return to the word of God?

To understand how America got here, a world history lesson is in order. From Babel, the cult of Semiramis migrated to the coast of western Turkey and mixed with Greek mythology. While this was going on, Israel was experiencing a time of great distress. The nation set apart to take God's eternal covenant to the pagan world, was compromising with the Phoenecian fertility cults in Jerusalem. Ahab and Jezebel were on the throne in Israel's northern kingdom.

Ahab was a Man who once knew the God of Abraham, Isaac, and Jacob. He married a Phoenecian woman who was the daughter of the high priest of the biggest fertility cult in the Middle East at that time. Jezebel first advanced the narrative that Jewish women should sacrifice their children on bronze altars where children were burned to please the god's of Phoenecia. Baal, Bel, Marduk, Ishtar and so on and so on. These same God's permeate the minds of American women who worship Hillary and Bill Clinton. They are the modern Ahab and Jezebel.

All the way down to the inquisition that they pulled on Vince Foster to seize a piece of land for their own use. They killed him just like Ahab and Jezebel killed Naboth and his family. This may be hard to take if you have voted for Democrats, but it is still the hard truth! Just like Israel, America began to worship the polytheist god's and imported them here.

The civil war brought Roman Catholics here in large numbers. They are the Church of Thyatira Jesus Christ recognized in Revelation 3. Thyatira is the Greek name of Semiramis. Roman Catholics more than any other polytheist belief system practice synecretism. The Papal coat of arms is adorned with the keys of Jannes and Jambres. These are the two Egyptian priests Moses dueled on the banks of the Nile. Jesus Christ intends to swallow their serpent also.

The Pope assumes the name of the Babylonian high priest for life. He claims to be God's man on earth, yet he allows nuns to occupy positions as temple priestesses. This practice emanated from Babylon not Jerusalem. It is pagan.

God commanded Adam and Eve to be fruitful and multiply. To convince women to live a life of virginity denies God's plan in the life of that woman. Pontifex Maximus is an abhorrent person to Jesus Christ. Catholicism has nothing to do with the death, burial, and resurrection of Jesus Christ. It cannot save a person. It will however separate a person from the Love of God through belief that God needs mediators between him and man.

Every practice of Rome was condemned in scripture by Jesus Christ. Whenever the desire arises for words to be written in code, the code writer must plan for hostile jamming. That is exactly what Jesus Christ prepared for when John penned Revelation.

Hostile Jamming of God's word occurs in churches across America every Sunday. The Protestant Church is no better. They are all married to the government, and the world. They are dead, and in need of true biblical Teshuva! Repent and return to the word of God alone not your pagan church!

God said he hates the Nicaolaitans. The cult was born in Ephesus under the deacon Nicholas. You can read about him in Acts and Colossians. He became a progenitor of Greek hermeneutics. He melded Christianity with the eugenic mind that says our way is God's way. He is the great grandfather to Saint Nicholas. He convinced Christians to support the pagan government in Rome by providing gifts for their children on the winter solstice. This holiday celebrates the new birth of the sun not the birth of God's son.

God commands us in Ecclesiastes to never celebrate the day of ones' birth, but celebrate the day of ones' death. It is on the day you die to mans' ways, to life in God's one way that you should truly celebrate.

Fear of dying is the complete opposite of faith in God's will and word. If you fear death, or sickness, or hell, you are not saved! If you spend more time worried about church and American traditions, more than you spend studying God's word, then you are not a child of God's kingdom.

Jesus Christ never celebrated his own birthday, Pagan's do. Jesus Christ would never celebrate the Roman ceremony of Eros. This is the only Greek word for love not in the Bible. Valentine's day is completely an abhoration to the God you claim to love and serve.

Easter venerates Jezebel's fertility cult and no longer has anything to do with the resurrection of Jesus Christ. If it did, you would crucify the bunny rabbit fertility goddess and be raised incorruptible in Christ alone. No need to give your children chocolate to win their favor.

We are condemning supposedly Christian children to a life venerating every holiday and tradition God hates. God said he hates the deeds of the Nicaoalitans. God hates religious traditions that usurp the death, burial, and resurrection of Jesus Christ. America leads the way when it comes to exporting everything God hates.

We in America live in a world that has been heavily laden with Greek eugenic thinking. The God of the bible practiced Hebrew hermeneutics when he gave Moses the Torah. God explains in Genesis 6 what happened to monotheism in the world he created. He allowed it all to occur to see if humans would ever believe the word of God.

We as the body of Christ are failing miserably. The rebellion of the Archangel Lucifer has led to synecretism and nowhere is it practiced so naively then in my America.

The same question posed by Lucifer in the Garden to Eve, the mother of all living was: " DID GOD SAY?" He is still getting Greek seminary educated pastors to answer the same way he got Eve to answer at the first human deception.

When a Christian replaces God's word with denominational church thinking, he can no longer use that person. He gave us his written word, and said this is the deal, not let's make a deal. God is not a 1980's game show host, he is the creator of our universe who died to raise dead men to life.

Church in America still teaches that God died to make bad men good. That is because they know not who Jesus Christ is! He is Immanuel. He is the Lion of the tribe of Judah. He is the second person of the creation Godhead. He is Adonai-Elohim. The Lord our God is one God.

Now that America has legislated for the deification of women, our children are condemned to a life laden with whoredoms and adultery. Divorce rates are higher in the denominational church than they are in abject Atheism. Semiramis laid the foundation for the current practices in America that God hates. Ahab and Jezebel continued those practices when they convinced our Hebrew ancestors to murder their children on fertility altars. These babies were the first Christian martyrs on earth. Nothing has changed.

Silent pulpits are the American anathema. The holocaust has migrated to America and Christians and Jews continue to vote for people who God hates. Our society professes to empower women while convincing them to murder their offspring and practice sexual immorality.

Christian parents reliant on Church tradition are all to blame.

I am one of those parents. I did not live my life according to biblical morality and the Roman church tradition of divorce and remarrying started with my Father and continued through my life and now my offspring struggle to make sense of what LOVE is.

I learned that women were an object of my sexual perversion, and I destroyed my Christian testimony. I thought I was entitled to sex, and the world around me cheered as I destroyed women's lives and glory!

Those were times in my life where my entire upbringing was being called into question. I was questioning my ancestry. I questioned my Roman Catholic upbringing. I questioned my thinking on all things dealing with morality. I was twenty-six years old. I had returned from the worst firefight in United States history following Viet Nam. My peers recited the Ranger creed, yet they slept with other Ranger's wives. I exchanged girlfriends like I exchanged library books. My entire belief about God was in jeopardy. I was completely confused. So, I began to read the Bible again for the first time since I was twelve.

The road has been loaded with moral landmines. It seems everyone liked me more when I practiced whoredoms. It was the bible alone that taught me God is married to his creation. The Gospel is one where God finds his son a bride forever. The dowry is paid in full. I am Christ's reward. I am his virgin gentile-Jewish bride. He will never leave me nor forsake me. Hallelujah!

God is redeeming his creation and the marriage covenant is God's teaching tool as to who he is saving. He is saving the Bride of Christ while the rest of the body of Christ will endure the great tribulation.

Church folk believe they are saved and they may well be, but if they do not divorce the world's thinking they are not the bride of Christ who will be raptured!

The Book of Hosea was written to the United States of America. We are the whore of the story. The nation that once knew God has married the Roman polytheistic system and we place their traditions and liturgy schedule ahead of God's foundation of mercy found in the pages of the Old Testament.

Jesus Christ did not worship on Sunday or on any of the Roman Church traditional holidays venerated and practiced by every Baptist, Every Protestant, Every Catholic and every other cult where people worship in three dimensional spaces for set periods of time.

God is the husbandmen who demands to be worshipped every hour of every day. And Jesus Christ will only be in the temple on shabbat and the new moons for 1000 Years! Hallelujah.

The Body of Christ must return to solid Old Testament preaching on mercy. We all need it if we are to be raptured. Ask yourself the Question? If I were Jesus Christ Be-trothed Bride to be, am I acting like the person I would Marry? Am I cheating on God through religious tradition? Am I acting like a virgin eagerly awaiting the bridegroom? Will I know my role in the coming kingdom? Would I make me the bride of the King? Repent and return to sound Bible teaching. It is our only hope.

Would God find his son a bride, and then beat her up during the 7-year time of Jacob's troubles?

He was crucified upon a cross of wood, yet he created the hill upon which it stood!

John Burns 7-28-2021.

American Naivete

Citizens of this country have lived in Geo-Physical comfort for 250 years now. The American march toward alternative morality is reaching its' end. God is intervening in the affairs of America and we Christians had better return to Biblical literacy before the opportunity for salvation evaporates.

The root of the problem was identified by Jesus Christ in his letter to Sardis in the third chapter of John's Revelation. The Lord Jesus Christ identified Sardis as a dead church. Jesus Christ died to produce death to one's religious trappings. His resurrection must lead to our own personnel resurrection. That resurrection must be grounded in humility. This requires we move away from church tradition and move toward total biblical literacy. To recognize that the death of denominational churches must precede any resurrection, is at the heart of America's future.

To rightly divide the word of truth as pertaining to Sardis, a geography and history lesson is in order. A proper Hebrew hermeneutical approach is also required for both John the Revelator and Jesus Christ are Jewish.

Greek was definitely the language of commerce at the time of Christ. However, both Jesus and John taught faith by using the Septuagint translation of our Hebrew Old Testament. We would do good to only use the Old Testament as our concordance.

The New Testament is in the Old Testament concealed and the Old Testament is the New Testament Revealed. Revelation is a singular pronoun. Revelation is transliterated as the unveiling. It is a singular book with a singular message.

The church in any form is in need of repentance if it intends to enter the coming kingdom of God on earth. A-millenial theosophy and replacement theology must disappear in favor of proper Hebrew hermeneutics. At the heart of the matter, is making God a Liar!

America is an incredibly Eugenic society. Every person who believes they are not prejudice, practice incredible prejudice in church every Sunday. Christians gather in all white, all Black, all Asian, heck name your poison churches! We preach a message of Christ love to only those who look like us. We form entire doctrines and theology based upon the color of our skin. This is ignorance to all things God in any form. Where did it all go wrong?

The Greek stoic philosophers believed they were the well born stock. Plato, Socrates, Sophocles all believed they were elitist powerful men who should control society and societies thought by telling people they are great, and people should only look to them for enlightenment about all thing's society should find great.

This thinking permeates every aspect of American life. Our politicians tell us they know what we need, our athletes tell us they are what we need, and our entertainers tell us they are the gods of this world. Add that to the color of skin and you have the perfect storm for race-baiting. The root of this problem began before Sardis.

The seven Churches of Revelation appear to reflect the order in which Church problems originated and evolved into our current denominational thinking. If the Seven Churches were addressed in any other order, my thinking would prove incorrect. Each Church reflects the Local, Homiletic and prophetic profile of 2000 years of Church History. They are all identified as Christ bride. Jesus Christ is male and each Church is identified by its' feminine pronoun name. It is a proper locative noun expressed in feminine pronoun form. This follows the paradigm established by God in the garden of Eden.

The Female was always supposed to be a suitable helpmeet to the male. He was always going to provide the blood covering for His bride. The male is responsible for the female salvation in any marriage covenant. God established that in the garden and he does not change!

Sardis is given the name that transliterates as Red Ones. This finishes the scarlet- thread paradigm begun in Genesis with Esau in the womb, through the Salvation of Rahab the gentile harlot, ending with Christ Church in Sardis.

This paradigm establishes God's intention to save his sons bride, by the blood of the Lamb of God in eternity past. This has profound repercussions in today's reformation churches. They long ago left the teaching of blood in favor of water baptism, speaking in tongues, and snake charming.

The prosperity doctrine advanced by wolves in sheep's clothing is coming to an abrupt end. America had her chance to flood the world with missionaries and money, but instead preacher's have horded incredible wealth within Mega- Churches who look good on the outside, but inside they are the problem!

No preacher should accept a wage for the message of Christ redemption. Paul did not, Peter did not and as far as I have gleaned, the wages of the First century preachers was **MARTYRDOM!** Only Judas got paid for the death ,burial, and resurrection of Jesus Christ!

The Church of Sardis is a reactionary church. It follows the pattern of progressive thought established by the Greeks. From Ephesus, to Smyrna, to Pergamos, to Thyatira, through Sardis, it has been a progressive move away from sound Old Testament Hebrew hermeneutics.

The book of Colossians provides incredible insight into the lives of the Gnostic teachers invading the known Greek world.

Sardis is the capitol of the ancient Lydians. It is where coins were first minted with men's pictures on them. It sits in the center of all Greek temples in western Turkey. Sardis is the center of the Roman-Greek world. Geo-physically it was dead center of all Greek temples in Asia Minor. Sardis was the center of trade routes and religious convictions. It is the place where Christ church become in need of resurrection!

Sardis, today, is the 19 main line denominations and every Church who was born out of Luther's reformation. They are all in need of resurrection according to Jesus Christ.

Every Denominational teacher has attended Seminary in some form. These institutions advance their agenda, not Gods' agenda. They are a my -way, or the highway group of teachers. They learned it during their education experience at American Seminary.

American Seminary purvey in Greek thought and wrongly identify Jesus Christ. Their overreliance on their education, reflects the lack of Holy Spirit anointing emanating from their pulpits. Christians live in fear of judgement. Faith ends at the door of Church. They annulled their marriage to Christ in favor of marrying government. Now their members await government handouts, and missionary outreach has morphed into legalism.

Outward piety replaced inward conviction. God did not die on the cross to make bad men good. He died to raise dead men to life! Hallelujah.

Sardis is the reason racism permeates every aspect of American thought. The Gnostics married Eugenics to Church thinking. Greek philosophy wrongly applied to Hebrew preaching.

It takes the Eastern Jewish mind to rightly divide the word of God. 87% of Bible content is Jewish thought. That is why Jesus Christ himself gave John the Revelation. The one who was raised from the dead, gave us the blood of the lamb to raise us all from dead denominational thinking.

Revelation is the word in English: Unveiling. The veil of the Jewish temple was rent in two when Jesus Christ died, because God was once again offering unfettered access to heaven through Jesus Christ our Jewish High Priest! The baptism in blood is the requirement for resurrection from dead religious traditions in favor of thus says the Lord.

God has raised up Messianic Jewish teachers of his word who Love Christ and were given the oracles of God. We all had better listen to them. The window of Western Greek thought has closed. The Hebrew language of Love is replacing Latin conquest languages in our worship of God's Jewish Messiah.

Sardis was on full display during World War 2. I have wrestled with my conscience over what was the greater tragedy of the Holocaust. The loss of life or the completely silent Christian and Catholic pulpits.

It was also on full display during the Kennedy administration forward to our current political debate. At the heart was eugenics. White Catholics knowing what every other American needed. The thing they got wrong was what they thought America did not need.

They believed America was better off without so much of the God of the Bible setting the moral compass for our nation. They embarked on a path that has left a breadcrumb trail to today's protests in our nations' capitol. Once again Sardis says nothing.

Pulpits listen to our President tell us what made us great was our money and our military. Those were the two Golden calves Jeroboam set up in Samaria and Dan that led to Israel losing its' national identity. I love the fact that our last President was taking on the Democratic establishment that led us here.

Their march toward chaos and total Biblical immorality had to be curtailed if America is to succeed. America succeeds only when the God of the Old Testament is glorified in our daily interaction with each other. America will succeed when it returns to Bible thinking. To do that our President must allow the Bible back in public school, for our children to access history, math, science and morality from a Biblical perspective.

If we do not, then the abandonment wrath of God is America's future. If we are not already there as a nation set apart to fulfill God's single purpose: Leading the world to a saving relationship with Jesus Christ.

Any time an American Christian hears the term globalist from a politician should read their Bible again.

There are two sides to any coin. On one side of the coin is human government. It is controlled completely by Satan. On the other side is the kingdom of God. It includes both the body of Christ and, the bride of Christ.

The body of Christ includes Old Testament saints and those who have died for Christ testimony. It includes the churches of Revelation. Only two are told they will not go through the tribulation that awaits human government and those who rely on it for their sustenance.

Only Smyrna, the persecuted church who endure martyrdom, and the Philadelphia missionary church who tirelessly take the Gospel of Jesus Christ to the fallen world every day, will be removed at the rapture prior to God chastening Israel for the last time.

The missionary church preaches the blood of the lamb cleansing us from all unrighteousness. The Sardisian Church of the reformation will go through the tribulation. Unless you get back under the blood, you will have one more shot at salvation: Martyrdom for the testimony that Jesus Christ alone saves you from your dead thinking.

If you sit in church on Sunday and do not hear about the blood of the lamb, then get out of that church and get back to the kingdom of Yeshua ha Messiah.

Churches hold God hostage, and never take him home or to our community unless it is in judgement!

Sardis believes it is their responsibility to rule the world through money and power. Sardis is where preachers purvey in fear. God is indeed a Globalist. But fear is not what he offers!

The fear of the Lord is the beginning of wisdom. Wisdom is found in God's word from Solomon in the book of proverbs. The wisdom that comes from God includes only two attributes, they are both divine attributes and should be what every professing Christian strives for in dealing with the fallen world. They are what God alone purveys in. These attributes make up God's entire Character. Mercy and Grace. They are not synonymous.

Mercy is the story of Israel the Nation as outlined in our Old Testament. Mercy is designed as the foundation of God's divinity. What makes him God is his eternal mercies. When David cheated with Bathsheba, and then conspired to murder Uriah, he plead with God not to turn Him over to men. For men are not able to show mercy unless they are under the blood of the lamb.

Mercy is to not receive what you deserve. The wages of sin, is death, but the gift of God is eternal life.

Mercy is what every person ever born of a woman needs every minute of their lives. To include after your profession of a saving faith in Christ.

David knew God from birth. He was anointed to reign at twelve. He killed a lion and a bear protecting his flock. Would your pastor kill a lion or bear for you?

David slew the giant by faith in Jesus Christ alone. He placed no faith in Saul's armor or government. Saul had already capitulated, and lived in fear of the enemy of God. David entered the Valley of Elah, with only the faith that God would carry out what Samuel had anointed him to do: Rule and Reign over Israel. The same destiny as Jesus Christ.

Modern Christians spend their entire existence without their two- edged sword by which they are commanded to slay giants for the fallen world. The Bible is the revealed word of

God the creator. Sardis does not help their church members remain under God's mercy. They claim to get people saved but never move on to Sanctification.

The Modern denominational Church perishes as their Pastors and congregations purvey in human wealth. Mercy is a requirement for grace to appear in your life today. If you are in the valley right now, then get under the blood of Jesus Christ and move on to sanctification in God's word every day.

If you do not have Jesus Christ, the smooth stone by which David slew goliath, the giant will slay you.

Poverty, unfaithfulness, sin.

These are the giant's God wants Christians to slay in the lives of believers. The fallen world needs Christians to practice Mercy again so Grace can appear. If not, Sardis fails and goes on to perdition.

Grace was God's answer to the need for mercy in Jerusalem. Grace is to receive what you do not deserve for free! Grace is the house the foundation of Mercy was established upon. God is building a kingdom, while Sardis continues to build churches.

God does not dwell in houses made with human hands. The Word became flesh and tabernacled amongst us. Jesus Christ is the house where Christians should place all hope in. He is available to all peoples. He does not need three-dimensional spaces to get people he loves his message. He is returning the church to its' Jewish roots, and methods for interpretation, and pagans are coming to Christ in the homes of their friends! Hallelujah.

The Gospel of Paul is being preached in workplaces, bars, nightclubs, and all over the globe! This is God's idea of globalism. The church should be embarrassed that politicians who never read the Bible, actually believe they know what God thinks.

To know what God thinks, they would have to experience God through the Bible. They have made themselves and their opinion gods.

The God that I serve is not willing to share his glory with me or them. I need his mercy and grace every moment of my feeble existence. I am praying for my country to return to God.

Government in any form has never, and will never wash anyone's feet!

Paul Gave us his Gospel in 1 Corinthians15. Jesus Christ died according to scripture. He was buried according to scripture. And he arose the third day according to scripture. This is the Gospel every human needs to hear.

The Gospel the reformation churches preach is tainted by denominational doctrines enslaving their members to doctrines not needed for entrance into God's kingdom. Only the Blood cleanses us from the sin that require God's mercy. Only mercy is required to receive grace daily.

The church needs to die to doctrine, bury their church dogma, and be raised incorruptible by the blood of the lamb. Then believers need to enter the word of God from genesis to revelation daily to find out if what I am saying is true.

America is dying to God and your repentance and return to sound Old Testament foundations of mercy will lead to America's repentance. We owe every person who has ever died for the testimony of Pauls' Gospel our repentance. This will take incredible courage. Will you take up your cross daily? The denominational church has a lot of market share, so losing revenue will perturb them!

- We live in the age of the church of Laodicea. The apostate church on earth. Long ago preachers argued for replacing God's people Israel. The Apostles went in search of temporal power and were martyred for their testimony of faith. To escape persecution the church married the world at Pergamos. At Thyatira, Roman pagans convinced the people to compromise with Paul's gospel and persecute the Jewish people throughout Europe culminating in the Holocaust. The Lutheran Church produced Anti-Semite Hitler. The Catholic Church produced Ahab and Jezebel and they have perpetrated an Inquisition upon all peoples 'of the Globe, and have amassed incredible wealth to present to their anti-Christian Pope. Sardis is where The church died and today it is dead still. Only resurrection will lead to repentance. Only Christ blood can cover a sinner from judgement by God and his messiah. Only resurrection will lead us back to missionary minded thinking in our communities.

- It is the job of every Christian to preach the gospel of Paul and his gospel came from the Old Testament.

- Paul wrote Corinthians around 58 AD. What Scriptures did Paul have?

I was born to a Roman Catholic Father and Jewish mother. My dad and mother divorced when I was an infant and I was in foster care. My Dad remarried and his new wife was agnostic at best, needless to say I have spent a lot of my life confused about God. So, I did what God wanted all along. Rely solely on His Bible and His promises for my salvation.

I learned very early that sin could never be covered by religious piety. Church can save nobody, and a church that does not preach the blood, is a mechanism of human government only. One more way to keep the mob from revolution.

I was introduced to Christ in The Army Rangers by my hero Dan Busch. He taught me that sin was not my problem. My problem is in how I expected to pay for that sin. Religion is the fig leaf Adam and Eve tried to hide their nakedness with. He told me that Church in any form had morphed into object paganism.

The Judeo-Christian Church completely in bed with government to get God out of our lives. It is time for Dan's courage to manifest in all of our Lives. If Dan could witness to me in the incredibly hostile world of Special Operations, then I have no excuses. Hell, no one is shooting at me yet for my profession of Faith!

I Love Jesus Christ. I have learned through faith in him to spend time with those who do not look like me if I am ever to learn Christian empathy. If I am ever to reach a lost world for Christ, then I must actually follow Paul's example, and enter the pagan world every day with my testimony of saving faith in Jesus Christ. To kidnap God in Church, and never take his message to the world, is failure on the church level. To not share your faith with people, is total failure on a human level.

I am married to the bridegroom of Creation, the Lord Jesus Christ. If I am ever to please him as his bride then I must follow his Biblical pattern. That requires I have the ability to lead people to him through the Old Testament eyes of mercy. If I do not judge people for sin, then God will not judge my sin! No person is without excuse.

To do what Jesus Christ did is to die to religious and government thinking. Sin exists in our members to teach us how dependent we are upon Jesus Christ our creator for our salvation. If your religious tradition is more important than Jesus Christ death, burial, and resurrection, then by all means keep God tucked away in church.

Resurrection begins when we acknowledge our need for God's mercy again in church and beyond! He was crucified upon a Cross of wood yet he created the hill upon which it stood! Even so come Lord Jesus Christ.

RLTW John Burns 6-7-2020, 76 years since Rangers Landed on Omaha Beach!

The Ephesian Dilemma

The Ephesian church is one of the two Church's to have two letters addressed to it. The First by Paul the Apostle to the gentiles, and the letter Jesus Christ dictated to the church's founder, and, writer of the book of Revelation. One of the sons of thunder, John the Apostle.

We will begin our study with the letter Jesus Christ dictated to an angel to be delivered and written by John. The seven letters to the seven churches, are the most important teachings a member of God's kingdom can rightly divide.

The word Revelation is singular not plural. It is one revelation of Jesus Christ true Church, as labeled by messiah as his bride. He being masculine, the word Ephesus is a feminine pronoun. It is understood as "My desired one". It is the apostolic church founded by John, and admonished by Jesus Christ and Paul.

Ephesus is a city on the coast of western Turkey in modern Izmir province. It enjoyed a geographic position as the center of pagan Greek worship. The temple of Artemis was in Ephesus. Artemis is Mother nature.

Greek life revolved around the veneration of created deities. Ephesus is the feminine goddess of fertility. Her roots can be traced to the cult of Semiramis in Babylon. She is most often depicted posing with reindeer, for she is the deity Americans call mother nature. John the Apostle set up shop in Ephesus after escaping persecution in Jerusalem.

Ephesus was first settled by the Lydian Greek colonists in the 14th and 13th centuries, BC. It is where the Greek life was full. There was a theatre, a gymnasium, a massive library, and the temple of Artemis. It was considered the most modern city of its' time.

Greek life in western Turkey was centered in Ephesus for a long time. It would be conquered by Cyrus the great who allowed for the worship of Artemis to continue. It would be re-conquered by Alexander the Great and Hellenization took on renewed life as he funded the construction of the city. At the time of John and Paul, Ephesus was the center of Roman life in western Turkey.

The ancient Jewish people had settled in Ephesus and at the time of the apostles, there was a prominent Jewish synagogue in the city center. This is a paradigm of our Jewish ancestor's fate as God chose to destroy their temple in Jerusalem, and send them packing around the entire globe. The diaspora begun in 70 AD is drawing to a close as I pen these words.

Israel is in the land and prospering, America finds itself under the abandonment wrath of Yeshua, and the Laodicean church has manifest around the globe. Where the carcases' lie, there the eagles shall be gathered.

Paul the apostle, lays the groundwork for the admonishment Jesus Christ would issue in Revelation 2. Ephesians 3;18 is Paul's remedy for the problem they had. Paul tells the church to allow their whole breadth, width, depth and height, to be sanctified to the will of God the father. The Church of Ephesus was only getting three of them right.

Depth, width, and Height are easy for most professing Christians to Sanctify. It is church, attendance and ministry outreach. But what about breadth?

The word breadth in the original Koine Greek translation was understood as a great expanse of time. To cross the breadth of the ocean requires a sea captain to spend a lot of time learning to navigate the entire breadth of the ocean expanse. Breadth to the Greek mind, has nothing to do with church, it has everything to do with how much time you spend alone with Jesus Christ.

Paul the Apostle laid out in Ephesians what God sees as true membership in his kingdom of Jew and Greek people's. John was remanded to issue the rebuke for what they were getting wrong. The Ephesian church was going to Church every week. They chose the Roman model for worship on the venerable day of the Sun. Sunday.

God's sabbath will always be Shabbat. Friday evening to Saturday evening. It is one of two days that Jesus Christ will be in the temple during the millennium. The other is the new moon. Sunday is the day the Roman Caesar's gave slaves the day off. Six days shall a man work and on the seventh he shall rest.

Sunday is the first day of the work week in God's Bible. It has never changed. Men changed in their haste to assimilate to Roman, pagan tradition's.

Ephesus is where many pagan traditions migrated into church worship services. Roman holidays began to be venerated by Ephesian Christians, and time spent earning income became more important than spending time with Jesus Christ. Alone in prayer and supplication with thanksgiving, and in the sanctifying work of the study of scripture.

This is why there is absolutely no power in the gospel being taught in today's denominational church's. They are ok with Roman holidays and church tradition started by our ancestors. They are fine with lukewarm Christianity.

Jesus Christ admonished the Ephesian church with the word's "YOU have lost your first Love". He was speaking to John the Revelator and an amazing recipient of the love of Christ. It is John who introduces the world to the Agape love of Jesus Christ. It is John who was entrusted with the care of Jesus Christ mother Mary. She is buried in Ephesus right beside John the apostle today.

Since Jesus Christ saw fit to entrust John with the care of his mother, and the admonition of the Church, he must also be the one who can provide Christians with the remedy to our dilemma.

1 John 5:4,5 is the remedy for those who have an ear to hear. Do you have an ear to hear what the Spirit is saying to the modern Ephesian church? For whatsoever is born of God

over-cometh the world: and this is the victory that over-cometh the world, even our faith. Who is he that over-cometh the world but he that believes Jesus Christ is the Son of God! Hallelujah!

The Ephesian letter is a letter that should give us Biblical hope. It was at Ephesus that Christ introduces us to the prophetic timeline of church history. Ephesus denotes the apostolic church age. It begins with the calling of the twelve, and ends with the martyrdom of Polycarp in Smyrna. He is the Bishop John anoints at Ephesus to be over the church of Smryna, and the second church Jesus Christ addresses in his letters to the seven church's. Smyrna is the place where gentile persecution begins to occur in western Turkey.

The Ephesian letter finishes with the practical application of Christian faith. We are commanded to put on the full armor of God. Having our loins girt about with truth, having on the breastplate of righteousness, our feet shod with the preparation of the gospel of peace, taking the shield of faith, the helmet of salvation, and the sword of the spirit which is the word of God. It has two edges.

At the time of the writing of Pauls' admonition to the Ephesian Church, Rome was the world superpower. The sword the Roman legionnaire would take into battle was the two-edged gladius.

Our Bible is one message with two edges over two testaments. Mercy is the message of the Old Testament, and grace is who appears in the New Testament. He has a Name. it is yeshua ha messiah or Jesus Christ in English.

He preached Salvation from a Hebrew hermeneutical perspective gleaned while he was writing the Old Testament in eternity past. He is the author and finisher of our Faith. He is the Lion of the tribe of Judah. He is the Alpha and the Omega, He is the Aleph and the Tau. He is our redeemer.

He is coming soon at the sound of the trumpet to retrieve his bride, and bring her to heaven to receive her mansion. He will return to this world with his bride at the end of the tribulation to receive his kingdom and inheritance. He is alive forever more. Hallelujah.

The Ephesian Church had become so adept at Church attendance once or twice a week, they were now ok with not spending time with Messiah. John could not wait to see Christ in the gospel period. After the resurrection, church attendance became more important than personal relationship to Jesus Christ. It was comfortable having people see you at church. Outward piety, replaced inward conviction. Jesus Christ is upset.

The one thing the Ephesians were getting write was that they hated any type of Church hierarchy. Relationship to God was personal. The Nicaolaitans were the precursors to the Pope, Bishops, Priest's, Deacons, and lay people who started a government where men lorded over the lives of believers. It was a cult started by the deacon Nicholas in Acts 6.

The words can be derived from two Greek words. Nicao: To rule over, and laity: the people. There is one mediator between God and man, the Lord Jesus Christ. Jesus Christ hates any type of church hierarchy where men set up other men who appear outwardly pious but inside, they are ravenous wolves. The only person to earn a wage from Christ crucifixion and gospel was Judas! Christ condemned the need for government in church.

The reaction of the Roman government was to begin wholesale persecution of gentile christians in Asia minor beginning with the martyrdom of Polycarp. It would not end until Constantine married government to the Christian church at Pergamos.

Persecution was the lot for professing Christians from Stephen through the current persecution of believers in Africa and other countries where government as God leaves believers in Christ with no other option than death. Are you willing to die for Christ testimony of himself? If not, then you are not justified or should I say, saved.

Even so come Lord Jesus Christ.

He was crucified upon a cross of wood, yet he created the hill upon which it stood.

RLTW John Burns 6-28-2021.

Biblical Tithing

America is under the abandonment wrath of God. Immorality has become mainstream, and everyone does what is right in their own eyes. The A-millennial Christian church has failed in bringing the gospel to a fallen world, and, their alternative message comes with no Holy Spirit power.

Churches in America, have accepted Satan's deception. They are more worried about losing market value than they are in getting people saved. They unabashedly follow the Roman calendar model, replete with synecretism, and all kinds of pagan traditions hiding behind their denominational titles and endless doctrines and dogma's.

In their quest for temporal power, they believe it is their job to establish an alternative morality than the one laid out in the pages of the Bible. I wholly believe Greek -minded seminary education is behind every shortcoming the church is facing. The reformation may have alerted the middle age church to salvation alone through faith with grace being the catalyst, however, it also gave us the Holocaust.

Silent pulpits are complicit in the mass murder of 6 million Jews and, 63 million deaths throughout the world during the second world war. Today, Christians rely heavily on Greek educated pastors to provide them with a moral compass direction from which to understand our future in Christ to their own peril.

We are warned as individual Christians that our future is in our own hands. Not one person will be standing by our side when we meet the Messiah.

God is not a socialist. He has patiently given every person born of a woman the chance to accept his preposterous debt payment plan, but his patience is wearing thin. Christianity was never meant to be a corporate event. God alone saves people, and he does it one soul at a time.

The Bible is the most amazing work of literature ever concocted. It was written in eternity past by a loving God who alone holds the warranty deed to each one of our lives. When a person sets out to study the word of God, I would suggest losing all presuppositions and all of your religious convictions, and wait upon God to remove the veil from your eyes.

As you embark on the greatest Journey of your life, your faith in thus says the Lord will enable you to experience God and his messiah. Church does a good job at providing order in society, but we are seeing church's close at amazing rates in America.

I have been to 45 countries on 5 continents. I have experienced every religious conviction on earth. What I have come to realize is they all bear the same fingerprint. They focus on three dimensional spaces from which to kidnap God for set periods of time, and in their haste, they have exchanged the worship of God as creator with the worship of his creation. The denominational church in America will not escape God's judgement.

The time has come for judgement to begin, and to begin in the House of God!

Pick your poison. God does not dwell in houses made with human hands. The Word became flesh and tabernacled amongst us, his name is Jesus Christ, and he is the God of creation.

Jesus Christ warned us all to be not deceived. That is exactly what has happened. It began in the garden of Eden, and was paid for in the garden of Gethsemane. Satan is the master of deception. He deceived one third of the angels in heaven, and convinced them to worship him. He deceived Eve in the same way that he deceives church members: He gets us to ask the question " did God Say"? and then rely on every book or teaching except the teachings of the Bible to answer questions about doctrine and dogma.

Joshua was warned to not let this book of the law depart out of your mouth, but to meditate upon it day and night, to be careful to do all that is written within it.

John the Revelator warned us to not add to or take away from the words of the prophecy of this book.

The Bible is one Book! It is supernatural in origin. It is the mind of God. It is the greatest Love story ever concocted. It is entirely prophetic in its delivery. It contains a personal message to every person born of a woman. You can find yourself in God's plan of redemption once you lose all religious presuppositions.

It contains the greatest mysteries of the creator and his creation. It is an algorythym written by the original Intelligent designer of the universe. It has encoded messages to you the reader, and outlines our past, present, and future in God's kingdom.

It is the single book the Messiah alone is able to open and interpret at the judgement seat of Christ. It is God's single plan for redeeming his creation, the terra Firma and us as the center of his creative plan.

Elohim alone is the greatest play-write in history. In the beginning was the Word, and the Word was with God, and the Word was God! What a Statement. This book that most of us have in our homes collecting dust and holding doors open or dashboards dust free, is the key to everything that happens in life!

And the Church was silent as the Supreme Court in 1962 removed our childrens' only weapon by which to fight evil from their education experience.

You want to stop school shootings: then return the Bible and prayer to our Children's public- school experience. The pulpits in America are entertainer and charlatan filled. Jesus

Christ did not die to make anyone wealthy. How do you justify hoarding immense wealth in church coffers while proclaiming that God alone will supply all of our needs according to his riches in glory?

The only fruit of the apostle's message was the fruit of martyrdom and the gift of God to allow us to take part in missionary outreach. Paul the Apostle worked as a tentmaker and tent repairer as he carried the Gospel to the entire Roman world.

Every Apostle except John, would die a Martyrs' death. Not one would die wealthy. We have supposed Christian ministries hoarding immense wealth while the homeless problem in America skyrockets.

Prosperity preachers have deceived their members into believing money is a seed, I find that nowhere in the Bible.

Jesus Christ proclaimed we are in the world but not of this world. All of our blessings are tied to the blood sacrifice of the cross. I just can- not fathom hijacking the gospel message in order to be wealthy in this life. Jesus Christ reminded the rich young ruler to sell everything and come follow him. You never hear about that man again. He chose monetary wealth and power over the message of Christ.

There is a financial plan outlined by God in his word. It centers around the tithe. It is singular in purpose and, possessive in nature. God reminds us in the book of Malachi to return unto God the whole tithe and see if I will not pour you out a blessing so big the world cannot contain it. The tithe is rooted and grounded in faith to believe that God owns everything including money. It is his already ,and he requires believers to participate through faith in giving God the first 10 percent of all of your increase. It is between you and God.

If you trust God with what is already his, he promises to bless the other 90 percent 100- fold. Wall street can- not give you the return on investment that God can. It is a simple way to take part in God's plan for the entire world. It will bring the peace of God that surpasseth all understanding to your financial life.

It is a supernatural faith. I have experienced God through tithing and not placing any emphasis on those things moth and rust decay. My life has gotten much better since I learned the biblical principal of tithing. The tithe is the first ten percent.

Anyone can give God ten percent of what is left over. It takes Holy Spirit faith to trust God with the first ten percent of your increase every pay day. Your finances will never be the same again if you faithfully find a ministry God is actually behind, and support it through faithful tithing.

The key is to let go of the tithe through faith in God. Prayerfully ask God to direct you to a ministry that is lining up with his perfect will in the Bible. Then trust God to bless the ministry, and provide all of your needs according to his riches in glory.

Jesus Christ gives us a prophetic overview of which church's will be raptured and which will go through the tribulation.

In Revelation 2 and 3, Jesus gives us admonition through the Churches of Smyrna and Philadelphia.

Smyrna is the persecuted church while Philadelphia is the missionary outreach church. They are the only churches told they will not go through the tribulation. To include the Protestant reformation church of Sardis which is warned that it is a dead church. It looks good on the outside but internally they are ravenous wolves.

The denominational church is in need of resurrection power. Water baptism, speaking in tongues, Church tradition, will all go down to perdition for those people who have not rightly divided the word of God. Careful study of the scriptures deals the death blow to all modern churches, who rely on things other than the blood of the lamb and the word of their testimony for salvation.

Adding anything other than what Jesus Christ outlined for the gentile church is heresy and blasphemy.

To make a doctrine that shackles men to dogma is not God's plan. Understanding God's entire plan outlined in the entire Bible is God's will for your Christian life.

Justification, Sanctification, and Glorification is the three-step plan into God's eternal Kingdom. A careful study of ecclesiology teaches us the uniqueness of the church in God's plan. The Church was founded on Pentecost in Acts 2. Everything that occurred in the life of Christ in Jesus walk on earth, was directed to a Jewish audience. He was the Messiah to the Jews first and that has never changed.

Just because they knew not the hour of their visitation does not mean God is not saving the Jewish people. Their inheritance and rewards are different than our gentile rewards and inheritance. God has not replaced Israel or it's people with gentile believers. To the contrary, he is saving them both.

Jesus Christ died for the Jew first and then the Greek. One day they will pray Hosanna, blessed is he who comes in the name of the Lord. They will look upon him whom they have pierced, and he will return to save God's bride along- side saving the bride of Christ.

The entire Bible is a love story concocted by Elohim in eternity past. It is the story of our marriage to God through the blood of the lamb and the words of our testimony. God hates divorce. He could never leave us in a state of separation from him, and that is why he concocted the most preposterous debt payment plan in history.

He is redeeming his people and his physical creation to himself. In the end we win! Our life on earth is secure through Jesus Christ alone. The Bible is the warranty deed for your life given by the creator of the universe. Just like buying a Ford, you want the warranty in the glove box to be from Henry Ford rather than rely on Chevrolet to fix your ford. You need the Bible to fix your belief system.

The Holy Spirit is one prayer away. The shortest distance between whatever you are facing and God's perfect will for your life is the distance between your knees and the ground.

Pray for Jesus Christ alone to bestow mercy and grace into your existence. Then open the pages of God's Bible and begin the greatest journey you have ever taken.

He is on the Throne forever, and His name is Yeshua ha Messiah.

He was Crucified on a Cross of wood, yet he created the hill upon which it stood! Even So come Lord Jesus Christ.

RLTW John Burns March 3 2020.

Jezreel

A word every believer in God should get to know well. It transliterates into English as that which God has sown. It is a city of the tribe of Issachar where wicked King Ahab and King Jehu spilled blood. It is Biblically relevant to America today as God has set up the kingdom of Jehu in the person of Donald Trump. God said he alone will avenge the blood of Jezreel upon the house of Jehu. The Psalm 83 war is upon us.

The recent peace plan unveiled by Jared Kushner requires Israel to once again cede land to the Muslim usurper Palestinians. It led to Benjamin Netanyahu losing his fight and a compromise was reached for him to be replaced by a very modern Israeli General in Benny Gantz. That did not happen in 18 months. Netanyahu has now been replaced with a secular Zionist, We exist in the times of Asaph.

Netanyahu is God's man to unite the tribe of Judah with the tribes of breakaway Israel, to unite the land for the first time since King David. It is all in preparation for the building of the Jewish temple in the city of David to receive Yeshua Ha Messiah.

For the temple to be Levitically purified to receive the high priest and covenant king the Jews were promised, the land must be united under a leader of the tribe of Benjamin. It follows the biblical paradigm for the last time the land was united under King Saul.

David followed Saul as the rightful leader of the tribe of Judah over the affairs of God's people Israel.

The Jews await two Messiahs': Yeshua Ben David, and Yeshua Ben Joseph. The bible reminds us he is the same king. His name is Jesus Christ.

I believe David was of the first-fruits' of the resurrection of Christ. He accompanied other Old Testament saints that came out of the grave with Christ in Jerusalem in 32 AD. I believe he will co rule with all believers in God's entire plan as outlined in our bible.

David and the church have a common destiny, and his name is Yeshua ha Messiah.

For Donald Trump to have been President at a time where his number one adviser was a Kaballah Jewish practicioner, is also following the Biblical pattern, and world History. Adolph Hitler too had a Jewish adviser who helped him carry out the Holocaust.

Alfred Rosenberg wrote the Myth of the 20th Century. It was the Nazi's primary doctrine of annihilation carried out upon God's covenant people. The second being abortion and eugenics introduced to the Nazi's by Margaret Sangar and Lothrop Stoddard. Both devout anti-semites. Both highly educated Americans.

These were elitist eugenecist's. Today, the modern Democratic Party is the fruit of their policies. The Nazi's murdered undesirables in the open, and the Democrats murder them in the sanctity of the womb of the mother. Cowards!

We should Pray for our country and our President. That is supposed to be the Christian and Jewish Way. God has reserved a remnant of believing Jews to carry out his purposes in the last days. I believe the last days began when the Jews lost their temple in Jerusalem in 70 A.D. For good or Bad, we will all serve Yeshua in Jerusalem during the Millenium.

The last to repent will be the Jewish remnant in Israel as they look upon him whom they have pierced, and cry out Hosanna, blessed is he who comes in the name of the Lord. This will occur during the last three- and one- half years of human government on earth.

Donald Trump has done more to advance God's agenda than any President in my life time. He has recognized Jerusalem as Israel's capitol, something every President promised but none delivered on. He has rolled back abortion and cut federal spending to the W.H.O. who during the recent Corona Pandemic announced that regardless of how many people die they will not use American money they have been given to fight it, because they would have to cut the global budget set aside for killing babies in the womb.

Jews and Christian Americans have been funding Democratic abortion agendas on the global scale to the tune of 20 billion dollars a year. He has sent stalwart diplomats to the United Nations to stem the Islamic agenda of destroying America's biblical foundations of government. He befriended church leaders and won the vote of the majority of white pastors in the last election. He has worked tirelessly to call America to pray for our country.

He has worked with the black community and created empowerment zones in traditionally impoverished black neighborhoods with 20 Billion Dollar a year grants to bring back the YMCA in our inner cities. He has been attacked every day by the Democratic party who refuses to stop their agenda, they are hell-bent on wiping out every semblance of Judeo- Christian values America has left.

He Has halted the Clinton global agenda in it's tracks. Ahab, Jezebel, and Jehoram have been halted.

The assault on the black community by the eugenic minded political elite, Democrats, has been halted for a moment.: But they will never cede power easily.

Hillary and Bill still are the democratic puppet masters. Barak Obama is a modern political W.E.B. Dubois who himself was a eugenecist. Dubois believed black procreation needed to be stemmed and stopped in inner cities and so does Barak Obama.

Where are the Martin Luther King Jr.'s when we need them? Dr. King believed in judging by the content of a man's character, and not the color of their skin. Yet Democrats never mention the character, and only focus on dividing us by the color of our skin.

Please pray for our nation to overcome racial divides. God created the human race with common ancestors. We are united in God through his Holy Spirit alone. It is politicians who get rich from enflaming racism, and it helps none of us.

America is on the cusp of being under the abandonment wrath of God if we are not there already. Teshuva is required. Repentance and prayer for God's mercy is the only course to God's grace. But I must mention that government in any form will never wash a man's feet. That is true separation of Church and State and it was Jesus Christ model for Christian worship. Has your Pastor ever washed anyone's Feet before collecting the offering? Just a Thought.

Donald Trump was called from his mother's womb for God's purpose, and perfect will. God has a permissive will, and a perfect will. God's perfect will is for all men to come to the knowledge of Jesus Christ. His permissive will has allowed our President to roll back some of Satan's agenda while failing miserably to get men to rely on God's provision, more than man's monetary system.

Just like Jehu he will fail at removing America's two Golden calves.

The bull of Wall Street in New York, and the bull of the Federal reserve in D.C. He has unabashedly advanced the agenda of the cult of Mithras hiding in plain sight as the eugenic minded Republican party.

They only want to help those with as much money as them. They wage a war to keep their cult in power.

Modern Pergamos occupies our White House, and always has. There have been a few exceptions over the course of history but none since Lincoln! Our country has indoctrinated Jews and Christians into reliance on government rather than reliance on God. Donald Trump had a very small window to roll back their Eugenic agenda. He tried, now our country will be destroyed for exporting everything God abhors. As Billy Graham once quipped what Thomas Jefferson felt: If God does not judge America he will have to apologize to Sodom and Gomorrah.

What do the paradigms' of the Bible tell us? It is never too late to repent and return to God. To return to God means to return to the teachings of the Bible. God is done with church in America. He has always been building a kingdom while men, built houses God has never dwelt in.

We are returning to the Acts of the Apostles when Jews and Gentile Christians worshipped God in their homes. Today if you hear Gods' voice harden not your Hearts. Today is the hour of salvation in Jesus Christ.

The Bible states that God avenges the house of Jehu upon Jezreel. I believe this is the future of America and Israel. Jehu occupied the White House at the time of this revelation. Our President is descended from the tribe of people known in the Bible as the Amalakites.

When Abram entered Canaan, they occupied the lands south of Jerusalem in the Negev Desert. I believe they were exported to Germany sometime during Titus Vespasians conquest of Israel in 70-74 A.D. The Amalakites were the first people to encounter The Israelites when they left Egypt.

The word Transliterates as Anti-Semite. The Nazi's executed at Nuremberg were all Amalakite's, following the Biblical ancestry of Haman in Persia. He and His sons were killed and displayed on crosses in Persia at the direction of ArtaXerxes Longimanus. He was the leader of the World at that time, and his wife was Jewish Queen Esther.

Jesus Christ prophesied of a delusion that would be poured out upon men that they would believe the lie. He said if believers were not sealed than they would follow the delusion. That delusion has been going on since the church was established in Jerusalem.

Jews and gentile Christians have lost their first love and prefer church and synagogue over faith in God's eternal plan for redemption contained in both Testaments of our Bible. It is time for Jews and Christians to cross the divisions brought about by unbelief, and return to the teachings of the Bible. Every Christian should require a pastor to lead them to Christ through the Old Testament alone, or I would go home and read my Bible with my family daily, and forget about three- dimensional spaces masquerading as God's church. He stands at the door and knocks which means he is outside of church not in it!

Our President had done what every President had done in history during their First term: work on re-election. Presidents reveal their true intentions when they win re-election. According to Jesus Christ words: Where the carcasses lie, there the eagles will gather. There has been more bodies lost to war in the valley of Jezreel than any place in history. Saul fell in Jezreel. Johnathan fell in Jezreel also.

Every traditional enemy of Israel in history has an eagle as their national emblem. The presidential seal at this time faces the olive branch of Israel and peace, but one day soon it will face the arrows of war.

An American President will turn on Israel for the last time. He will be the man of lawlessness out of the west who unites the Satanic trinity of false prophet Pope in Rome, with an Assyrian Anti-Christ. Jerusalem will be their target, and to exalt himself above everything called God will be their agenda.

There are seven I will statement's given by Lucifer himself in Isaiah 14 that echo every despotic leader in world history. Pride always comes before the fall.

America was proud after 9/11 and returned to rebuilding the tower God had allowed to be thrown down. We relied on the God of fortresses to avenge our losses on 9/11, and sacrificed thousands of our men and women in the Middle East and beyond. I know. I was friends with a great number of them, and my soldier bloodline was joined to them in the constant struggle that Christian soldiers bear more than most: To return to a country that has tried to destroy the faith that got them home from war!

I believe in the Idea of America from a Biblical standpoint and I have finally found what is really worth fighting for. I pray Donald Trump is not who I suspect he is, and will repent and get Americans to return to subsistence farming and get the Bible back in public school so that our children will once again have their weapons to stop school shootings: prayer and the word of God. This would truly make America great again.

The Bible has a Lot to say about the times we are living in. For every scripture of Christ's first appearance there are seven that remind us of his second coming. The oldest prophecy in the Bible comes from Enoch : I seen the Lord coming with ten thousand of his saints. Hallelujah. We are commanded to eagerly await the coming of Christ and to Pray daily for the salvation of every person born of a woman. This includes to pray for our President to call upon Jesus Christ for guidance during these times.

I pray He is being Biblically advised by someone other than a western educated, seminary indoctrinated pastor. I pray he has a son of Issachar telling him the times and seasons as they pertain to Israel. I pray he advises the Israeli prime Minister to take the Palestinian territories and cleanse the land of all pagan idols to include the Roman Catholic Church's shrines' established by Constantine's mother.

A time of great persecution is coming upon the body of true believers in God's plan of redemption. Satan is losing , his time is short, and American Christians will not escape persecution. American Christians will die at the hands of both political parties.

As Christians we should be neither Democrat or Republican. A two- party system without God could only ever produce corruption. As Christians we are Monarchists who believe in A risen king who is returning for his bride. He is the way, the truth and the life. His Name is Yeshua Ha Messiah or Jesus Christ in English.

He is only coming back for those who are looking to him as Lord and Savior. All others are entering the time of Jacob's trouble as prophesied in the Bible. America will turn on the Jewish remnant, and God will turn on America.

To achieve the Trump peace plan for Israel they have to tunnel through Hezekiah's well. It is the only water source presently controlled completely by Israel. It will be used by Jews for the ceremony required to purify the Levitical priests prior to the dedication of the coming millennial temple.

There will never be another innocent lamb sacrificed in Israel! The lamb of God was slain, and the Jewish remnant will build the structure but a couple things are missing from the original design for there is no longer a need to shed innocent blood.

Israel must never accept this plan. If they do, then the rapture is right around the corner. I will be watching from the mezzanine level in heaven. Even so come Lord Jesus Christ.

RLTW John Burns 4-25-2020.

He was crucified upon a cross of wood yet he created the hill upon which it stood.

Learn the Parable of the Fig Tree

Why did Jesus Christ teach in Parables? To answer this question, we must determine who did Jesus Christ come to, and why did he come to Jerusalem in Israel. The amillennial Church has fumbled the ball terribly in understanding the great commission, and the role of the Bible in the lives of Believers.

When Paul the Apostle wrote 1 Corinthians, he had entered a predominantly Hellenized Roman world. Rule was absolute. The biggest fear emanating from Caesar in Rome, was the fear of religious uprising. Rome moved quickly to stamp out any new religious movement.

The Pharisees and Sadducees, with, all of their differences, still took their orders from the Jewish High Priest. Paul was in Jerusalem to witness the beginning of Apostolic ministry to the Jewish people. He was present when Stephen gave the greatest Bible lesson on how God views his prophets, priests and kings.

He explained through the lives of the patriarchs, and Moses, how they all failed the first time, and through the leading of the Holy Spirit were successful the second time. Paul explained to us that the Gospel he preached was straight out of scripture and had three elements.

Jesus Christ Died, Jesus Christ was Buried, and Jesus Christ rose from the Dead: and all according to scripture. What scripture was Paul referencing?

Corinthians has been afforded a 67 A.D date of earliest writing. The Gospels were not in circulation in writing in 67 A.D. so what scripture was Paul referring to? Any serious student would have to conclude that PAUL, as an educated Roman Jew, who was taught by the most venerated Rabbi in the Roman world, Gamaliel, only had the Septuagint translation of the Hebrew Bible as his only viable conclusion!

It would be Paul who would teach us in Ephesians, that we are to put on the full armor of God and to take with us the Sword of the Spirit. The sword we are to wield is the word of God.

And out of his mouth, went a sharp two- edged sword. Jesus Christ, our Jewish Messiah, rightly identified his word as being one sword with two edges.

The Old Testament is the story of the bloodline, and nation, that would give birth to our messiah. It is the story of God's unending mercy toward the Jewish people.

The New Testament is the story of the Messiah born, to save the world from their sins, and to eventually sit upon the throne of David forever. It is a literal earthly throne in Jerusalem. God has once again turned his attention eastward, the trumpet will soon sound, and the dead in Christ will rise first, and we which are alive and remain, will be caught up to meet him in the clouds.

The word of God has gone forth to all the nations of the earth. The Jewish remnant is back in the land and prospering. The Psalm 83 War is upon us, and this event is a Biblical prerequisite to rebuilding the temple. The land of Israel must be cleansed of all pagan temples and all unbelievers before the Temple could be consecrated.

Jesus Christ is coming back to the Mount of Olives after the tribulation of the last 42 months of gentile reign on the earth. The bride returns with Messiah to rule and reign over all the nations of the earth during the millennium. Those who received crowns at the marriage supper, will receive kingdoms to rule and reign over, beside Jesus Christ and King David.

We will worship Jesus Christ as King, for 1000 years in the temple in Jerusalem, on Shabbat, and the New Moons.

This wisdom could be gleaned by Christians, if, their pastors would shed religious traditions, and return to thus says the Lord!

The Old Testament is where we find the reasons for needing mercy. Mercy alone is Graces foundation! Without mercy, grace can- not overtake a man or woman seeking Christ. Mercy is not receiving what we all fully deserve: for the wages of sin is death. We all like sheep have gone astray. This does not end when we accept Christ, it only just begins.

Paul reminded us that after many years in ministry he is still chief amongst sinners. I need God's mercy every day.

When I acknowledge my shortcomings, and ask God for mercy: Grace appears in the form of Jesus Christ. I repent and return to saving grace only because of God's unending mercy. Only because I understand the story of my ancestors in the Old Testament.

I personally, will not sit under the teachings of a preacher who can- not lead a person to Christ using only the Old Testament. If you ask me why I will say this. It is because neither did Jesus Christ!

The Bible is one book revealed to at least 40 men, over 3000 years, saying the same thing on every line and page! It is the greatest algorithm ever produced, and, it came completely from the God of Creation before he spoke our world into existence. Line upon Line, line upon line, precept upon precept; precept upon precept. Here a little, there a little. Here a little, there a little. And he spoke to us in similitudes and metaphors, as holy men were instructed to, by the God of our Bible.

The Bible is the script of the master play-write. We are the actors playing out the cosmic love story with Elohim as Romeo, and we the virgin bride grafted into the Jewish vine as Juliet! Hallelujah!

How do I know I am right about AMILLENIALISM? Because God has once again chosen to use a JACKASS to warn his people of his imminent return, and their need to understand Jesus Christ coming kingdom from the Bible perspective.

Matthew 23 gives us a view into the heart and purpose of God creating us in the first place. Verse 37 reminds us all of the trajectory of all human history; how God had wanted to gather the Jewish people together as a hen gathers her chicks, and they would not; which leads to the tragedy of all human history; behold, your house is left unto you desolate.

In 70 A.D. Titus Vespasian would surround Jerusalem, and, starve its' inhabitants. Rather than surrender, and trust God's providence, the Jewish priests set fire to the temple. Titus in anger, raised it to the ground.

God would allow the Jewish remnant who survived, to be transported to the entire four corners of the Roman world.

It continued through the immigration of Spanish, and European Jews, into North America following World War 2. This will lead to the triumph of all human history: When the Jewish remnant in Jerusalem during the Tribulation looks upon Him whom they have pierced, and cry blessed is he who comes in the name of the Lord!

God Wins!

Salvation is of the Jew first, and then the Greek. That has always been Gods' plan. God never replaced Israel with gentile Christians. Rather, he used gentile nations to hide his believing remnant until these last days of the regathering in the land of Israel, for Christ to redeem in Revelation 5.

The Christian Church must repent and begin to rightly divide the word of truth!

At the heart, is to understand the uniqueness of gentiles born after 32 A.D. who call upon the Lord, and are saved. Just because God changed his attention does not mean he changed his focus. He has allocated mercy upon the Jewish remnant throughout the gentile church age. However, he had always wished they would accept grace in the form of Yeshua Ha Messiah. Jesus the Christ.

God's mercy is something the Christian church has forgotten. Jesus Christ himself requires mercy and not sacrifice. The church moved further, and further away from Old Testament doctrines. I believe, it was a result of the reaction to persecution in the early apostolic church in Jerusalem.

As Stephen was martyred by religious minded Jews who denied Yeshua as messiah, and King, they emigrated into the Roman world, and began to incorporate their churches into the Roman solar pantheon.

Christians began to deny sound Jewish doctrines given to us by God in Genesis.

John the Revelator was taken behind the veil of creation, and given a prophetic profile as to the direction the church would take in moving away from the Jewish doctrines Jesus Christ followed during his life, toward the replacement theology most denominational churches ascribe to today.

Leviticus is the book from which Jesus Christ practiced his calling as The Jewish High Priest.

God's calendar has never changed. It is the 360- day Babylonian calendar. Knowledge of this calendar is the only way for Christians to understand God's prophetic plan for humanity.

Prophecy is to understand Bible patterns. It is not prediction. Every event in Human history that matters to God, is recorded in the Bible. He has laid out the end from the beginning. He uses paradigms to teach us he has never changed. While the church changed, God did not!

Today in America, professing Christians gather on Sunday, to kidnap God in mighty houses for the worship of ideas that are not scriptural. The Bible was given to us to guide us down the believing path toward eventual Glorification in God's kingdom.

To get there, a return to sound Old Testament teaching is required by the God who has not changed. His entire prophetic plan for Israel is unfolding right before our eyes, and I wonder how many church going people know God's plan for our brothers, and sisters that have Jewish bloodlines.

The believing remnant is returning to the land from the diaspora. Jewish believers in Yeshua Ha Messiah are starting churches in Israel. The land of our messiah is fast getting ready for his imminent return, and Christians in America need to require their pastors to return and repent: Teshuva!

We live in a time the Bible says more about then it says about the time Jesus walked the earth! Yet Christians refuse to be sanctified by the word alone. Continuing to rely on amillennial preachers, educated in eugenic minded Greek seminaries, and only dividing the body of Christ as it was divided on the Cross.

Denominations practice incredible prejudice. They believe like the ancient Greeks that their way is the way to God. They deny God's attribute of omnipresence, and try to kidnap him for two hours on the wrong day of the week.

Sunday is the day God began his work known as the creation. It is the first day of the work week for God throughout eternity. If you are preaching on Sunday then your gospel is a gospel of works, then go ahead, accept wages from the tithes, and offerings. You have your reward!

Not by works lest any man should boast. Every word, every letter, every proverb, every Psalm, was designed by God. Jesus Christ reminded the apostles, that not one Yot, or one tittle, would disappear from the law, until all should be fulfilled. Is all fulfilled?

Is Jesus Christ ruling, and reigning from Jerusalem? Is the sheep and goats' judgement proceeding from his throne in Israel? Has the bride of Christ, been raptured? Is martyrdom an accepted doctrine of the church in America? Why should American Christians escape what Christians worldwide face every day?

Persecution was the only fruit harvested in the church until Constantine married the church to the Roman pantheon of fertility holidays, and solar calendars. Endless church doctrines trying to prove your church's way is the only way.

Learn the Parable of the Fig Tree

Every denomination adds to the finished work of Christ on the cross.

Putting Christians in bondage to every church tradition, while not sanctifying them through the Word of God.

We must become Berean Christians, straight outta the Acts of the Apostles! We must find out if what John Burns is saying is true, and, we must do it alone. God, went out of his way to get his people a message, and most believers hold their bedroom doors open with it. The Bible collects dust, while our children are indoctrinated into Darwinian evolutionary beliefs in public school.

We rely on public school teachers to instill morality in our children. Well, those teachers were educated in the indoctrination factories know as universities and colleges in America. God has been removed from our children's education experience, beginning in kindergarten. Teachers have not been taught Gods will since 1963!

Darwin tells your children that they began as cosmic goo. That goo became nothing, and then nothing exploded billions of years ago. From that goo and explosion came your beautiful baby girl or boy. I find it easier to believe "Beersheeht Bara Elohim et Shamayim et Erets!

In the beginning God created the heavens, and the earth. From that simple belief hangs all the promises of God ever debated! To know Elohim as creator, is the question of all eternity.

To know the creator of everything ever created, to include men and women, entered our dimension of time, and space, in the womb of a Jewish virgin, to die on a cross of wood, for the sins of humanity; PAST, present, and future.

To be raised from the dead to place believers on the path to sanctification, and proposed glorification in eternity future. To know Elohim did it all to reward Jesus Christ with the Bride of Yeshua ha Messiah, and, his inheritance of the kingdom of David in Jerusalem, brings me PEACE!

I have traveled many miles in this life, often alone in the flesh. People may have been there, but I was traveling in ten dimensions. God exists in eternity! He is the God of time who created all space. To know the God of time is to understand life, for the fear of the Lord is the beginning of wisdom.

To fear God as creator is the duty of every person born of a woman. To gain knowledge leads to understanding. understanding is how we apply what the Bible say,s in accordance with God's will for our life. To understand that God has a permissive will, and, a perfect will, is the duty of every believer in Yeshua.

His permissive will allows Satan to rule over the seven super kingdoms on earth to include America in all of her glory.

His permissive will has allowed the Denominational church to portray him as a liar. God has never replaced Israel! The church is unique in its' purpose.

God is saving the nation of Israel, and his tithe of land, and, he is reversing the curse.

Jew and gentile will receive the same grace. Knowing the difference between inheritance, and reward, would fix our denominational thinking. God could no sooner divorce Israel then he could divorce the bride of Christ! Both have lost their first love!

It has always been the blood of the lamb, that cleanses us from all unrighteousness, to include the unrighteousness of denominational thinking, God has always been the Way, the Truth, and the Life.

God's name is Yeshua Ha Messiah! Jesus Christ is the English rendering of his providential name Elohim.

It takes a lifetime of studying to show yourself approved, and to come to this Holy Spirit filled conclusion. To begin the journey takes the faith to take the first step. The first step is to understand God the creator had a plan for your life, and it is in the Bible.

Your life is in the Bible. You have to be willing to find yourself in its' pages. I suggest starting a journal and write in it every day. When I am asked where should I begin, I say: Revelation, for it is the only book that promises a blessing to the reader for just reading it!

Revelation, from a study perspective, holds the distinction of requiring you go through every other book in the Bible to uncover its meaning. There are 404 verses with 800 allusions to Old Testament truth. To rightly divide the word of truth requires you understand that division requires at least two of anything.

I would start by believing the Old Testament is revealed in the New Testament while the New Testament is concealed in the Old Testament. God was concealing his message from an un- anointed fallen angel. He is not the author of confusion to those who believe; however, he designed his word to keep Satan on his toes.

The battle is between God, and the Nachash, or shining one: Not you and I!

God provided a way for us as Humans to return to him, and it is the most preposterous debt payment plan in history. A simple wooden executioners' cross, with a willing Lamb crucified upon it, frees the believer from the knowledge we owe God our lives to pay for our sin debt to him.

The wages of sin is death; The gift of God is eternal life through Jesus Christ our crucified, and risen Lord!

Of the Jew first, and then the Greek! God is not done with the fig tree in Israel. Even so come Lord Jesus Christ.

RLTW John Burns 2-50-2022.

He was crucified upon a cross of wood, yet he created the hill upon which it stood.

GRACE

Socrates Once Quipped

It may be that deity can forgive sin; I just do not see how? Where did a western, Greek, philosopher, from the sixth century B.C., glean that knowledge? Deity to the Greek's, centered around the pantheon of god's that emanated from mythology. Their mythology was born out of a belief, that a rebellion occurred in another world that led to a fight between men and the god's, with immortal deities being birthed as a result. The offspring of men and God.

Zeus was one of the god's birthed out of this heavenly battle. He was born in the temple town of Pergamos. The temple high priest, Pontifex Maximus, had accepted a human baby sacrifice, and the altar at Pergamos was superheated to accept the offspring of women. The babies were thrown on the bronze altar, and Zeus was born out of that sacrifice.

Where did Pergamos come from? In Etymology the word Pergamos is made from two Greek words: Per which means unholy, and gamos, which alludes to marriage. Jesus Christ identified Pergamos as the seat of Satan on earth. The people who serve at its' temple, he called the synagogue of Satan.

Revelation two teaches us how Jesus Christ feels about Pergamos and its' future.

Pergamos is the city where the Christian church married the world system, and it occurred before John had his Revelation on Patmos. The unholy marriage between church and state is alive and well in America, it functions from the modern city of Pergamos: New York City.

In Geography, Pergamos is a city on the Western coast of Turkey. The temple of Pergamos was built by the Lydians who settled the coast. The Lydians are an ancient peoples of traditional Greek island explorers. They settled western Turkey sometime between the 8th and 9th centuries B.C. They ruled western Turkey until 585 B.C. with their defeat to Cyrus the great.

Like every ancient city, they enjoyed a founding mythology that is still debated today. What should not be debated is the religion born out of that mythology is being practiced in America today. The capitol of Lydia was the town of Sardis. About 26 kilometers from Pergamos.

Two distinct people groups were wed at Pergamos. The Persians and the Greeks. Warfare always leads to settlement by conquering forces. As Cyrus settled Anatolia, he would have assimilated with Greek gods while enforcing the worship of the Persian pantheon. This is the pattern of Antiquity.

All Ancient pantheon of gods and goddesses can be traced to Babel and their ancient high priest Nimrod. From the marriage of Nimrod to Semiramis, we get the entire pantheon of moon god marrying solar deity, then coupled with divination by watching the stars.

Babel is where creator worship was replaced with the worship of the creation.

Man established a system of priests and priestesses to worship the heavens and the earth. Nimrod was high priest, Semiramis was the high priestess. Through adultery, Semiramis would birth Tammuz and she would hide her infidelity by proclaiming she was a virgin, and the birth of Tammuz was a result of the creator god, Baal, visiting her, and giving her a son. Babel is where the church married the state in antiquity.

Nimrod is the worlds' first dictator, who also became the leader of the national religion based upon the worship of everything in the creation. The world that then was, married the new system of worship, and the word religion first appeared in our etymology.

The marriage of east and west is the oldest religious proposal man has ever offered. Today it is charachterized by treaties of western civilization with eastern civilization for the purchase of oil. At the center is the compromise of eastern moon god worship, with western worship of the solar pantheon.

Caught in the middle, are Christians and Jews who worship the creator more than worship his creation.

Jerusalem is the center of Elohim the creator's world view. Every language east of Jerusalem is written from right to left. Every language west of Jerusalem is written from left to right. The religion of eastern peoples' centers around the 360-day moon calendar and lunar pantheon. The focus of every government of western peoples' centers around the 365- day solar calendar and religious pantheon. The desire for eastern and western peoples to conquer and rule each other can be traced back to Babel and Nimrod.

It was here at Babel that the monotheism first taught by Enoch was changed to polytheism by men in search of temporal power and wealth.

Enoch was the first teacher of Astronomy. The plan of the creator was first etched in the heavens in eternity past. All peoples could go into the darkness of night and gaze skyward to view God's plan of redemption. The twelve constellations of stars that permeate our night sky, were viewed by all ancient cultures between the equators, and they are without excuse.

God the creator has always planned to redeem his creation. His battle is with the original rebel; Lucifer. The leader of the creation's oldest rebellion against God. Isaiah 14 and Ezekiel 28 confirm that God's battle is from before he created the earth inhabitable for humans. His battle is with the Nachash of the garden of Eden. The shining one Lucifer: The anointed cherub that covereth.

He is one of the three Archangels God had created to lead worship in heaven. He is identified as the most beautiful thing ever created by God. His clothing was twelve precious stones. His only job was to lead worship in heaven. He was asked a question by God himself? Would you rather reign in heaven or rule on Earth? That is the same question God asks every person born of a woman. Lucifer is still asking humans today.

Lucifer was not alone in his rebellion. He was getting the angels in heaven prepared to receive God and worship him, when he decided to sit on God's throne and demand the angels worship himself. One third of the angels bowed down to worship Lucifer, and the first rebellion is recorded in heaven itself.

This led to angelic warfare in eternity past. Jesus Christ teaches us that he saw Lucifer fall from heaven like lightning. He fell to the earth that then was in eternity past and the Bible does not specify when. We know it is earth where he is cast because he shows up in the garden at the first temptation of Adam and Eve.

He asked the question did God say? He is in the church today asking the same question and they are still failing to answer with God's answer. Instead, they continue to build churches while God builds a kingdom based on the principal of time and not three- dimensional space.

The denominational Church long ago married Pergamos at Sardis and they will go through the tribulation, and they are in need of resurrection, as Jesus Christ labeled them a dead church.

God follows the Old Testament liturgy schedule in Leviticus. He has never changed. He celebrated Passover when he lived amongst us. He celebrated Pentecost, the feast of unleavened bread, the feast of dedication, and he worshipped God in the temple of Jerusalem on Shabbat not Sunday.

Shema Israel Adonai Elohim Echad Adonai. Listen oh Israel for the Lord our God is one Lord.

He has never changed, and his calendar was established in eternity past. Julius Caesar changed the calendar to suit the solar pantheon, and the church is fully in bed with government every time they celebrate Roman holidays.

Caesar was the first Roman Emperor to adopt the Babylonian title Pontifex Maximus. Today the Catholic Pope adopts the same title. The church in all forms has married the world and there is a future price to pay.

I am an insurrectionist! I follow the model of Jesus Christ. I teach salvation from an Old Testament perspective. I speak out against government in any form that mocks the God of the Bible. I intend to hold religious leaders accountable for marrying the world system long ago. I intend to pray for my extended family to receive God's messiah and enjoy immortality.

The marriage of church and state has been completed in my lifetime and it manifest in the form of a two -party system in America. As noted in the Bible, a two- party system will never get you into heaven. God's two parties involve recognition of what he alone calls good and evil, not men disguised as American politicians telling you what you need in this life.

God alone is all you need, for if you really had God there would be no need to depend on government in any form. Government will never wash anyone's feet! A two- party system could never deliver anything but lobbyists and corruption. And they have fooled the people who claim to know Messiah the most.

When a new President is elected, he becomes Zeus, the head of the political party in power. The party who has the majority becomes the high priests and priestesses to carry out his wishes. The entire Greek system, adopted from Babylon, migrated into the Roman model and today western Greek thinking permeates the minds of politicians everywhere.

It is a Eugenic model advanced by Socrates, Plato, Sophocles, Demas and many other Greek philosophers. It was present when Alexander set out to conquer the Persians and Egyptians. Upon his death, Ptolemy united eastern and western thinking, and the result is the cult of Roman conquest that inhabits the minds of every world leader.

If you do not understand just look at the national emblems that emblazon the flags of countries around the world. Not the national flags but their battle standard. They are all emblazoned with the eagle clutching the serpent in some form, and some have double eagles, signifying their desire to conquer East and West to unite Babel again.

The goal of every world leader to include our American president is to unite east and west to stop God's plan of restoring absolute rule in Jerusalem. Jesus Christ will eventually have to step in as a modern Assyrian unites east and west to march on Israel, and try to stop God's plan of redemption.

Redemption includes Jerusalem being reestablished as the home of monotheism on earth. I believe the garden of Eden and the garden of Gethsemane, are the same place. God's preposterous debt payment plan was established in Eden when he prepared lamb skins to cover the sin of Adam and Eve. And he told us he was going to do it when he created the heavens and the earth in the beginning.

This begs the question, why was man ever created, if God was dealing with a rebellion in heaven? Well, God alone is absolutely holy. From his perspective, he alone should be worshipped, for he alone can- not lie. It is obvious to me when I read the entire Bible, the first thing that I have to confront is that God has an incredible sense of humor.

The fact that he created us with the ability to choose between worshipping him as creator, with choosing to worship the creation, is astounding to me. Why would God create humans with the same defect as Lucifer and the angels in heaven? Because he never changes! Hallelujah!

We have changed from time immortal, yet the creator has remained the same. His requirement for membership in his kingdom has never changed. To believe that because he is a God who takes responsibility for his creation, nothing but the death of God himself would ever bridge the Gulf between God's holiness and our ability to sin. And he did it all because he loves you and me. If I was the only one who ever needed redemption, God would have done it anyway.

I once imagined that the God of creation had placed me in the garden he planted, watered, and nurtured for my eventual sustenance. I then imagined he brought me to the center of the garden where he was tending a single tree. He gave me all the other trees from which to feed myself and all of the animals but the one tree was his alone, and I could not even touch it or else I would die.

I had absolutely no concept of death from God's perspective so immediately a sense of fear came over me. What does it mean to be dead in God's eyes? Then God gave me an assignment to name all of the animals he placed on earth to inhabit for his pleasure and our teaching.

As I was naming the animals, they began to reproduce and I became jealous there was no one for me to reproduce with. God, in an incredible act of mercy, puts me to sleep and takes a woman from my heart for no other part of the body causes us so much turmoil in relationship to our helpmeet.

So, I escort my new wife to the tree in the midst of the garden where she is confronted by the serpent with the question did God say? And she touches the tree that belongs to God. This is the question Lucifer uses to pose the question of which church should I attend? They all have their own version of what God said.

This is the question that led me on this lifetime journey to finally be answered by the entire Bible, and it alone would I acccept as God's plan for my life.

Men will always do what is right in their own eyes before looking to the one book that will always lead you back to the narrow path that leads to salvation. That narrow path is

God's tree in the garden. Man was supposed to tend all the trees but this one, for it was God's tree and it would have a specific time to be revealed by God in human history.

So, after the fall of Adam and Eve, God showed mercy and grace. He clothed them and banished them from the garden until a future date in time. He mercifully punished them in distinct ways befitting of the reasons he created them. Man would no longer have help tending the garden. It was up to him to till it and water it.

By the sweat of his brow, he was ordered to bring forth sustenance. If you are a man who will not work than you should not be allowed to eat!

Eve would experience pain in childbirth. I believe it has more to do with raising children from the female perspective of grace as their real punishment. Grace should be born out of empathy not sympathy when raising children.

Empathy is born out of human experience and can only be taught by failure not success. Mothers need to tell their children what they need to hear, not what they want to hear. Fathers are responsible for mercy. Mercy is defined by God as spanking your child when it is appropriate to fit their offense.

Little boys should be spanked more often, for life will spank them more often if they are not spanked.

We end up with single parent households with one of God's attributes missing when this pattern for parenting is not followed. Men are providers and protectors, and women are educators and the person responsible for telling the husband what he needs to hear. God is holding him accountable for the entire families' salvation, so respect your husband when he decides little Johnny or little Susie needs Godly correction.

Our children are suffering immensely in America because inside church is where the majority of divorces occur.

Men and women in America are being forced to make decisions that are not new to society, the speed at which society moves has changed. Just like the speed of light, it is no longer viewed as constant by the true scientific community. Morality is no longer viewed as absolute or constant, so men and women need to revert back to the true north of God's creation. It has never changed.

From eternity past, through the creation processes that made our world inhabitable, to todays' moral collapse in society, God intended to pay for his creation his way! It is the most preposterous debt payment plan in human history. That the God of creation, would leave his dimension of time, and enter our world in the womb of a Jewish virgin girl. He would experience every human frailty and remain sinless throughout his life while enduring the greatest sin which is to deny that God loves us unconditionally. Jesus showed just how much God loves his creation. At a set time he endured the cross of Calvary.

Who was responsible for Christ crucifixion? Christianity has blamed the Jews for two -thousand years. The high priest was unable to find one of the 613 laws of God in Leviticus that Jesus Christ broke. Pilate could find no Roman law that Jesus Christ broke. 6 trials he endured and they were all illegal and still Jesus Christ never opened his mouth to defend himself.

When the lamb is taken by the lion it never opens its' mouth. All the while God was teaching me metallurgy from the garden to the Roman empire. He taught me to forge weapons of warfare and three nails for the eventual torture apparatus.

At a set time he had me the sinner cut down the tree he has been watering since the garden was planted in Eden. He had me fashion that tree into a cross and take those three nails he taught me to forge from the iron he created. Then he had me whip him, insult him, spit upon him, and lead him to the place of the sacrifice.

He willingly laid upon the cross I had fashioned, and he said nothing, as I looked into his eyes and drove the nails into his hands and feet. I then raised him up for all the world to celebrate the crucifixion of God himself, who entered our world as the son of God and the son of man. To bear the sin debt for everyone born of a woman who should be called to believe. Do you hear him calling? Hellelujah!

I pray you hear my words, for God and I want you in his kingdom. It is the kingdom of David promised to Mary for her son for all eternity. It is a kingdom of the Jew first and then the Gentile believer who hears the still soft voice of God and says yes Lord I would rather serve in heaven than reign on earth. When you answer God, your life will never be the same, and you become immortal in God's image from the beginning. Hallelujah!

Greek thinking permeates our lives and has led America down the path of eugenics. race, creed, religion, fraternity, all lead to the well born stock thinking that haunts America. It is taught from grade school through secondary education. No wonder they fought to get the Bible out of public school. The Bible is the only book from antiquity that acknowledges we are all descended from a common ancestor family. No races in God's economy, only one human race.

That family was flawed in the eyes of God so God did the responsible thing and paid for the debt. The only debt that matters when you die is your sin debt to Elohim our creator. Jesus Christ became the propitiation for the sin debt of every person ever born of a woman.

From Adam to Cain. Cain murdered righteous Abel, who brought God a lamb to sacrifice for his sin. He understood God's plan and Cain killed him. But God had mercy and grace on Cain. He marked him with the Hebrew letter TAU, which is the symbol of the cross, and did not allow anyone to murder Cain for he became God's messenger to a fallen world.

Through one man's death, righteous Abel, God managed to get his message of salvation to an increasingly pagan world through Cain the guilty party. Gods' saving grace on full display. Abel was the sacrificial substitute for the sin of Cain. Without the shedding of blood, there is no remission for sin. Cain and Abel were rehearsing for the substitute of Christ for Barabbas. Hallelujah.

It is time America gets back to solid Old Testament mercy and escape the legalism that comes from the church selling the grace of the gospel. Jesus Christ alone is qualified to judge the sins of others. My job is to show mercy and grace through the anointing God has placed upon my life. That anointing requires I marry my experience in failure, with the mercy and grace God showed when he saved me, one person at a time.

Monotheism requires a belief that God alone is God and his name is Jesus Christ. He is the ELOHIM of creation. He is pre-existent in all matters to do with our natural world and its' order. He holds creation in the palm of his righteous right hand. He is our future king, and it is time for true Christians to accept that we are to be monarchists that speak out against a government that has legislated God out of our children's lives.

We must return to the Pergamos John the Revelator encountered, only this time we must be willing to die for our confession of faith rather than submit to a government that has no interest in fulfilling God's plan of redemption. His plan includes the redemption of the Jewish people and the return of the kingdom of David which will come about on the heels of the psalm 83 war.

The land of Israel is God's tithe at creation. He gave us the rest and sanctified Israel to himself. The church had better rediscover it's Jewish roots before it is too late and they find themselves left behind at the rapture. The only path to God post- rapture will be martyrdom at the hands of the religious leaders who have compromised, and their government bent on stopping Israel from building the millennial temple. This temple is the one Jesus Christ will return too.

I have much to say about the Church's identified as Jesus Christ Bride in Revelation 2 and 3. I have chosen to speak about Pergamos and Sardis because they are the two who have permeated my existence along- side Thyatira, the Church of my nativity and upbringing. These Churches more than any have led us to Laodicea: The apostate church. God anointed me to be a watchman over his people Israel.

I happen to believe everyone in Gods' kingdom will be accounted as Israel. In etymology God renamed the deceiver Jacob Israel: One who wrestles with God and wrestles with men. Is that not all of our fates? Do we not all wrestle with men and God when we question other people's convictions?

It is the Job of the Bible and the Holy Spirit to help you get back on the narrow path that alone leads to salvation. The path is one of belief, in the death, burial, and resurrection of Jesus Christ on the 14th through 17th of Nisan in 32 A.D. It was established in eternity past that the creator would die to pay our sin debt. The sooner you make the decision to believe that question, the easier life will become when tribulation and persecution come, for God alone is the God who comforted us once and for all on the cross of Calvary.

Teutelestoi !! Paid In Full! The last words God our Messiah spoke while suspended between heaven and earth upon a cross he created, he watered, he allowed me to cut down and nail him too. For it was all of our sin that nailed Jesus Christ to the cross to include the sin of religious tradition replacing God as creator who died to pay our sin debt.

When the Pharisees, and Sadducees, with Caiaphas, had come up empty. When Pilate found no fault. When the crowd hollered crucify Him! They all turned to religious tradition. To release a guilty man in the eyes of God and the Roman law, in exchange for a prisoner deemed to be at odds with the religion of the day, and causing the Roman government nervousness. A sinless God man would be exchanged for a murdering insurrectionist!

The plight of every person born of a woman. An exchange program. Your sin for his death! Your Guilt for his innocence. Your freedom for his confinement. Your life for his life? Choose life in Christ! This is the greatest choice A western educated, Roman soldier of Jewish descent through my mother, ever made!

Greek thinking permeates our lives in America. Our government, our schools and our houses of theology and theosophy, our churches. It is time we get back to Jewish hermeneutics and away from Greek eugenics. Greek was the language of commerce at the time of Christ advent, while Hebrew was the language Yeshua would have used to address his Jewish followers.

When addressing gentile's he changed to Aramaic. The Language of the common Roman legionnaire would have been Koine Greek. His commanders would have spoken Latin which is a conquest language. It is a language descended from the Greek nobles. So, in essence, Latin descended from

Greek, and merged with the many places Rome conquered along the way.

English is a combination of German and Latin. It is today the language of commerce for the known world. The American dollar is the reserve currency of the western world today. Our computer Algorhythms' have united all tongues and joined us in consolidating SIN under the modern Babel language; social media worldwide.

The fallen angel who led rebellion in heaven, and formed the basis for all ancient pantheons to worship the creation, is marshalling his forces for the last time. Israel and Jerusalem are their prize. They will stop at nothing to halt the plan of God. God sent a judge to America to warn us to repent and return to God! Teshuva!!!

He was crucified on a cross of wood yet he created the hill upon which it stood.

RLTW John Burns 7-30-2021.

Losing a Friend

What parameters designate someone as a friend in your life? Are you able to call yourself friend to anyone born of a woman? What attributes should one possess to be called a friend? Who is the greatest example of friend in human history? What did he do for us his friends? Does your Faith in him produce an ability to die for our Friends? Is my faith grounded in being his friend? Is friendship part time?

As a lifelong student of the Bible, I must turn to who Jesus Christ is to understand God's parameters for calling one his friend. I must glean from the two-edged sword of God's word the revelation that God has always been seeking friends!

He lost his best friend in a rebellion in which iniquity was found in him. Lucifer, the anointed cherubim that covereth, demanded to be worshipped by God's heavenly host of angels. He ascended to the throne of God, and in an instant, he fell from heaven like lightning. But not before instituting the first rebellion in Gods' history.

He successfully convinced one-third of the angels to bow and worship him, instead of Elohim the creator. Lucifer and his cohort of fallen angels have been laying down minefields in God's creation from the beginning. His goal is to keep anyone from becoming the friend of God.

Lucifer was created by God to be worship leader in Heaven. That alone is Gods' desire for every person born of a woman. To be his friend. To be God's friend, he demands worship. To worship God is to believe in his preposterous debt payment plan. The distance God was willing to go, to gain us as a friend is unrivaled in mercy and unmatched in grace.

No religion, doctrine, dogma, schedule, denomination or works, can equal just how far God was willing to go to have us become his friend. It takes complete surrender! Lose all pre-suppositions about God's demands, and focus on what he did for us, and not what we do for him!

God's religion has always been one of complete surrender to his plan of redemption.

Lucifer's rebellion advanced the plans of God set forth in eternity past, when the Trinity first gave us creation. God does not react He saw it coming!

He created Lucifer so beautiful, pride filled his being. He convinced one third of the Angels to look at his beauty by abandoning God's majesty. It permeates the modern Church experience.

To Look at Church tradition more then look to thus says the Lord requires repentance and return to sound biblical epistemology. Friendship to God has always required surrender to thus says the Lord. The Bible teaches us God has always been seeking friendship with his creation, and his creation only needs him when things are going wrong.

Most Christians have been touched by the birth of Jesus, but never transformed by the crucifixion and resurrection. That is why their friendships and marriages are failing. Jesus has become one more form of entertainment.

Christians are ok languishing in church. They are ok with believing Jesus died to give them the right to be God's moral compass. They judge everyone who does not submit to their denominational theosophy. At best they are gnostic heresies. At worst they are a deliberate attempt to liquidate every truth about Jesus Christ reward and Inheritance.

It is antisemitic to deny God's plan for Israel. Jesus Christ is coming back as a Jewish King and yet most of the church exchanged sound Hebrew interpretation techniques used by him for telling us who he is, and why he came, for Greek pagan hermeneutics.

They all meld pagan liturgical calendars with a little bit of Jesus! They are neither hot nor cold. That means they are lukewarm. Jesus Christ identifies the reformation church as dead and in need of biblical resurrection. Lukewarm Christians will be spit out of Jesus Christ mouth.

Denominational thinking has morphed into abject paganism. Blasphemy! The church married to the world. Pergamos on full display.

To be the friend of God, one must submit to belief in God's irrevocable covenants found in the Bible. Genesis 2:24 is the marriage covenant between one man and one woman for life. It sets forth the paradigm of God married to his creation. To be God's friend, one must submit to the bridegroom and be sanctified as the bride of Christ, through the washing and cleansing of his eternal word.

Malachi 3 reminds us of the purpose of the covenant of marriage: To produce Godly seed. It is through this Godly seed, that God planned to redeem the world. The virgin birth was acting out the plan of God becoming man in the womb of a virgin Jewish girl. And all for the purpose of dying on the Cross to redeem creation to God.

First, humans who accept through faith, God's debt payment plan. They are redeemed by the blood of the Lamb of God. It alone cleanses a sinner from unrighteousness. It is the longest blood transfusion in history. All for the purpose of God gaining us as friends.

However, it falls to us to gain God new friends. That will only occur when the church returns to evangelism in the homes of family and friends. Every church written of, or to, by John or Paul or Peter or Jude or James, met in believers' homes out of fear of Roman persecution.

Three- dimensional spaces for kidnapping God are a middle age phenomenon that emigrated here to America. God does not dwell in houses made with human hands.

We are called to be shepherds and we should learn from the shepherds of the Bible to know how God requires lambs to become lions before he calls them to shepherd his flock. The lion pride is absolute. The male lion who is over the pride, will only mate with one dominant female for life. He purposely runs off the juvenile male pride members so they can fight for their own pride outside the family dynamic. The pride male lion requires the other female lionesses to hunt and provide for the pride until they are plucked away by a male from another pride who has been banished in hopes he will fight for his right to mate, and start a new pride.

Pastor is taken from the Hebrew word for shepherd. David was the family shepherd. He had killed a lion and a bear before he turned twelve in defense of his flock! Would your pastor fight the lions and bears of this life, that actually cause us to lose faith?

How many pastors have been married multiple times? This is the first of God's covenants under attack in American churches every Sunday. Teshuva, repent and return to the first century word of Jesus Christ. Ask for mercy, and grace will overcome you!

The Second covenant under attack is the Abrahamic covenant. He who blesses the descendants of Abraham would be blessed, and he who curses the descendants of Abraham would be cursed. Replacement theology has kept the church from being blessed as a community of believers. To teach that somehow God replaced Israel as a nation, for a pagan church experience, is heresy.

Jesus Christ reminds us in the book of Matthew, that Israel would return to a marriage covenant with YHWH Elohim during the last days of the gentile Church age described in the book of Revelation. May 11, 1948 should put an end to middle age Thyatiran doctrine, where the church actually persecuted Jews and Christians for millennia.

The Roman Catholic church in their thirst for temporal power, consolidated the church as government. It is mystery Babylon, and the mother of all harlots. The first harlot she birthed was the Lutheran reformation during the Sardisian church age.

Martin Luther became virulently antisemitic. The Lutherans and Catholic Pope were responsible for the rise of Hitler and fascism. Silent pulpits will be dealt with at the rapture, when millions of people will go through the tribulation of the last day's as God judges the churches who exchanged belief in Jesus Christ as creator, for Roman church traditions and holidays.

Synecretism is to meld two religious belief systems into a way of life. God is a monotheist. To be his friend you should celebrate the holidays he celebrated when he was dwelling with men. He did not celebrate his birthday for it would violate his word in Ecclesiastes 7:1. He was the Passover lamb, so it was natural for the lamb to present himself four days before the crucifixion.

The last supper is the Passover seder meal. Jesus Christ would have partaken in the three cups before the fellowship meal. The cup he did not drink from is the seder cup of remembrance to remember the tearing down of the temple under Nebuchadnezzar.

Jesus Christ did not drink from the cup while the temple of Herod was standing. It was a usurper temple. He will drink of it when he comes into the kingdom after the 7 Year period of tribulation coming upon the Earth.

Jesus Christ would have rested on every Shabbat while he lived. He was a Jewish Rabbi who came to the lost sheep of Israel. He is wanting his bride to once again become the friend of national Israel. Then the church will not be attacking the Abrahamic covenant of Genesis 12.

Jesus Christ celebrated the feast of dedication, today referred to as Hannukah. The temple the Jews celebrated being dedicated was the 2d temple dedicated after the Hasmonean revolt of 168 B.C. when Antiochus Epiphanes had desecrated the altar in the holy of holies by slaughtering a sow upon the altar.

The temple he would celebrate, is the millennial temple where he will dedicate it himself. He alone will be worshipped as Lord and king over Israel, and God's rule will once again be over his creation for 1000 years.

If you are the bride and friend of God, then get on his bible program established at Berea. Study the word daily to find out if what John Burns is saying is true.

The Third covenant under attack is the Davidic covenant of 2 Samuel 7. When David is anointed by Samuel to inaugurate the dynasty of the tribe of Judah. Unlike the northern kingdom which had multiple dynasties, Judah has only ever had one.

From the line of David through Mary we have the Messiah and king being born. The Church attacks this covenant when it teaches the kingdom is only a spiritual kingdom. 87 Percent of scripture must be denied to come to a conclusion that the kingdom is happening now.

Jesus Christ was promised in the womb to sit upon the throne of David for 1000 literal years. It is a kingdom where Jews and gentiles are joined in belief of Yeshua ha Messiah. It is Governed by Jesus Christ and his bride of Jewish and gentile believers gleaned as the harvest during the church age. It has its' capitol in Jerusalem.

The Temple of men becomes the temple of our God once and for all. The sheep and goat's judgement will take place from messiah's throne in Jerusalem. David will carry out justice and mercy. There will be no darkness only the light of Christ. No sun or moon to worship for they disappeared during the great tribulation. The stars are all gone, they too fell. Only God and those who love him partaking in a kingdom governed by Jesus Christ as God- Man. Hallelujah.

To deny Jesus Christ future kingdom on earth denies the rapture. God always removes the righteous before he hands out his wrath upon men. Enoch, Lot and his family, Elijah, Naomi, Jesus Christ ascension, the Jewish diaspora, and finally the bride of Christ during the Laodicean church age.

We are in it! We have made our money and our military our gods. Too proud to request God's mercy, and too scared to preach his grace. One must die to religious tradition and be willing to suffer persecution as a result of your testimony that Jesus Christ alone can pay my sin debt to God.

Believe in the coming kingdom of our messiah. Pray for the peace of Jerusalem. Eagerly await his return in the clouds to sound the trumpet to remove you from the wrath coming upon the world of unbelievers.

The harbingers of coming judgement have all manifest in our lifetime. America is under the abandonment wrath of God as predicted by Messiah in Revelation. To know where America is in the bible, one must read no further than the book of Hosea, and America can no longer see the error in our ways.

We have played the harlot as a nation.

We have prostituted our Judeo-Christian heritage in exchange for the gods of polytheist nations.

The United Nations denies Israel's right to exist, and yet America still sends her Christian sons to die on battlefields where the gospel is forbidden. We have treaties where India captures an entire sector of our service industry. They own every gas station and hotel between San Francisco and Philadelphia. 6 of every 10 American dollars goes to India, never to return to the American economy.

Our government speaks out against the evils of sex trafficking and slavery, yet India still practices both on a humongous scale.

We tax our own citizens to the point where they have to choose whether they can afford to support missionary outreach or not. Taxing people who love God to pay for programs he abhors has brought the judgement of our God and creator. To legislate God out of our lives and halting our children from praying for their classmate's salvation is Luciferian and the denominational church has been completely complicit to gain favor with the Government. This Government will eventually divest from Israel and we will be destroyed as a nation. The Church must adopt a doctrine for complete support of the Jewish homeland promised to Abraham and his descendants forever.

The Palestinian usurpers have occupied the 7 principal cities from before the time of Joshua. God ordered them killed to the last woman and child.

The Nephillim were worshipped by the Canaanites. They will return soon to defend their satanic ideas for God's land. Israel must take the territories to prepare to build the millennial temple. They must finish the conquest of Joshua, and destroy the Satanic usurpers.

America has fallen and failed to repent. We have had 19 plus years of protracted war with no end in sight. We have not returned our nation to the bible. We have not asked for God's mercy so grace will no longer be shed on thee!

I weep as I come to these conclusions about the America I love and have defended. I can- not support a government that attacks my faith in Jesus Christ. I can- not support a government who emigrates people of polytheist belief systems here while not requiring their assimilation.

They bring their god's values which are at odds with our GOD! I can- not support a government who denies our children access to the bible, the only book used by the Puritans and later founding fathers to draft the documents from where we glean our laws. I can- not support a government who unjustly taxes wages which are deemed by the constitution to be private property. I can- not support a government influenced by lobbyists and not influenced by electors. I can- not support a government that has created a political elite class of people who will stop at nothing to increase their own wealth, and hold onto power. I can- not support a government that has lost sight of what it means to serve. I can- not support a government which sanctions my belief that Jesus Christ alone provides all of my needs according to his riches in glory.

I will never support a government that supports the destruction of Israel. I will never support a government that purveys in chaos to increase budgets and steal money. It is the Church's job to take care of the poor, not the government. Transferring the wealth of millions of poor people to people who are even poorer all the while paying themselves millions of dollars in congressional salaries and expense accounts transferred onto the backs of American taxpayers. We have created a government of, for, and by the people who always intended to get God out of our lives in order for government to become our God.

It is time to return the debate toward God again. He is America's only hope. The window is open for only a short time longer. The breath of God will soon return to him for a season, and the Holy Spirt will no longer be available during the final 7 years of gentile reign on earth.

God will poor out the delusion, and the body of Christ will cling to their Roman religious traditions and fertility celebrations to their own demise.

Biblical Teshuva is required on a global scale. The march toward biblical illiteracy has reached its' zenith. God has raised up sons of Issachar who know the times and the seasons as they pertain to Israel. We are living in the days of Asaph, and soon the psalm 83 war will commence, and the entire world will unite in the stopping of God's plan for Israel and her coming messiah.

America will unite the eagle's world- wide in the hatred of Israel and her Messiah. Where the carcasses lie, there the eagles will be gathered. Hallelujah!!!

The Final covenant under attack on a global scale is the messianic covenant of Jeremiah 31;31. The Messiah of Israel was to be born of the root and offspring of King David. He was to be a priest and king in the order of Melchisedec. He would save his people from their sins.

He was raised from the dead by the power of God. The Trinity is the only acceptable form of mono-theistic worship. Everyone is attacking the blood covenant established at the crucifixion of Jesus Christ in Jerusalem on Passover on Nisan 14 32 AD. They all Deny Jesus Christ as God and God's Messiah.

Islam, Hinduism, Shintoism, Tsaoism, Communism, Socialism, Sexism, Racism, Classism and on and on… America has gone the way of Baalim. The Church is silent. Abortion is the supposed law of our land, and Judeo-Christian taxpayers are on the hook for its' cost worldwide.

Pastors, preachers, teachers say nothing. They continue to kidnap God on Sunday and Wednesday with no intention on questioning government, religious leaders, or family members who violate God's covenants in Church's all across America.

Christian soldiers being asked to fight wars in pagan nations where our government has no intention of allowing proselytization of the gospel of Jesus Christ upon our arrival. Soldiers have been asked to choose God or country for the first time in America's history, and we are not winning the hearts and minds of Muslims anywhere.

Indian people arrive here in droves and end up owning a Gas station selling us all kinds of things that they themselves would never eat or drink. They own every hotel I have stayed in over the last ten years. The money I paid them in room costs has funded one very wealthy family in India, the Patel's.

India has a caste system where Christians are part of the lowest caste. They are required to work as slaves for very wealthy Indian billionaires and millionaires while most of the population lives in abject poverty'. Yet, our American politicians have negotiated these trade deals in order to have India co-sign on America's debt. India is half of the Asian equation as to why we no longer have manufacturing in middle and rural America.

Our Politicians have given them to populations of foreign countries who have neither our Judeo-Christian values or our moral conscious. It is time for American Christians to fully back God's Biblical plan of spreading the gospel. It requires we never miss an opportunity to share the reason for the joy that is within us. His name is Jesus Christ and he saves his people from their sins. He Makes a friend of anyone who believes he died to pay their sin debt, and he was resurrected to raise us all from dead religious thinking and a return to complete biblical literacy.

God provided himself as a lamb to remove the penalty for sin in our lives. It is the first step in the redemptive process if we are to inherit the kingdom promised to Jesus Christ in Mary his mother's womb. The second step is sanctification which removes the power of sin over our lives. To be sanctified to do God's will one must search the scriptures daily to find out if what I am saying is true. God gave us his word before he spoke the world into existence and that is what makes him God.

The Old Testament teaches us exactly why we all need God's mercy daily. The New Testament is the story of the God-man promised to mankind before the foundations of our universe were spoken into existence. It is the fulfillment of the promise to provide grace freely to everyone who would believe God died to pay our sin debt.

The New Testament is in the Old Testament concealed, and the Old Testament is the New Testament revealed. Every word pointed to Jesus Christ. God always planned to replace the friend he lost in heaven, Lucifer the Archangel, anointed to lead the angelic host in heaven, with humans who would accept his plan of redemption.

When you accept Gods' testimony of salvation contained in the Old and New Testaments of our bible you become the friend of God forever. You begin the journey toward eventual glorification and the removal of the presence of sin at the rapture and 2d coming in his millennial kingdom.

Justification, Sanctification, Glorification. The acceptance of God as Messiah and King, ensures you will only ever be called the friend of God.

God alone becomes the reason you live. Your marriage to Jesus Christ ensures friendship to Elohim as creator forever. No double jeopardy in God's kingdom. It was not the nails that held him to the cross it was his love for you and me that held him there!

He was crucified upon a Cross of wood, yet he created the hill upon which it stood.

RLTW John Burns 8-1-2021.

Practicing Synecretism

Synecretism is the melding of two belief systems to make a religious ideology and subsequent denomination or sect. No- where is it more on display then in America. Every holiday we venerate in America are pagan at best. I am the Lord your God, there shall be no other God's before me. Yet we welcome the foreign God's into our houses of worship and we do it on Roman calendar schedules.

The Christian church followed the pattern the ancient Hebrew's followed that led to the abandonment wrath of God upon the nation of Israel. Why should America escape what God's chosen people have endured for 2000 years now? The denominational church is under that abandonment wrath as I pen these words. I am the Lord and I change not. Forever…

Ecclesiastes 7: 1 says it is better to celebrate the day of one's death more than the day of one's birth. Jesus Christ never celebrated his birth, for he came into the world to die not live as a pagan worshipper of fertility deities.

Human beings are brought forth from the womb for the purpose of one day receiving God's messiah, Jesus Christ.

To be born once means you will die twice. You will die a physical death upon the end of your days on earth. If you never answer the still soft voice of God, ask you to accept Christ death as payment for the sin debt, we all owe God, then you will experience the second death which is eternal separation from God our creator.

When you accept Jesus Christ as savior, God has dealt with the penalty of sin in your life. Salvation begins to become a reality. With that salvation God expects a saved sinner to become an evangelist. God saves no human born of a woman for their own purposes. God is single minded and he needs us to share our testimony of salvation with the dying world around us.

If you confess Jesus Christ as savior then do not do it with vanity in mind. Do it in the spirit of thanksgiving, and know that God intends for you to take part in ministry wherever you find yourself.

Jesus Christ never celebrated the pagan belief to acknowledge the day of one's earthly birth. Jesus Christ has always been concerned with the new birth achieved when a human being cries out for mercy. Mercy is to know that you deserve death for the sin in your life. Mercy is built upon humility and empathy for sinners. Jesus Christ did not die to give us the right to judge others in this life. He died to give us the opportunity to look in our mirror, and every day realize without God's mercy, sin is real ,and I exist in the presence of sin. This humble knowledge requires mercy every day of our Christian walk.

God's answer to a sinner who asks for mercy is always grace. Mercy is to not receive what we deserve from God, for the wages of sin is death. We are born into this world for one purpose alone. Train up a child in the way they should go and when they are old, they will not depart from it. Does your child realize they were born to receive and subsequently serve God in saving sinners? Do you worship the birth of your child and then teach them to worship each other?

Which holidays did Jesus Christ take part in during his ministry to the lost sheep of Israel? The beginning of the Hebrew calendar that God actually follows is the Hebrew month of Nisan. Jesus Christ confirmed he was born on the first of Nisan when he said I am the first and the last. The month of Nisan is the first month of spring in Israel. The lambs that were born for the purpose of being ritually sacrificed in the Jewish temple, are all born in the month of Nisan and they are only born in Bethlehem. This pattern has never changed. Lambs are still born in Bethlehem, and still only in the month of Nisan in spring.

Jesus Christ was not born in December, and he never celebrated his own birthday. It was his death that would save sinners, not his birth. Jesus Christ was born as a lamb, but his future required him to become a lion.

Nisan 10 is the day that the lambs to be sacrificed are presented to the priests in the temple. Jews would travel to Jerusalem, and have their lamb inspected for worthiness to pay the temporary debt incurred by God's people for their sin. Jesus Christ himself traveled to Jerusalem on 10 Nisan in the

Year 32 AD to be inspected by the priests for worthiness as their lamb. He did it while riding on the colt of a foal.

The reason he rode a colt is because he was a willing son of God ready to pay for the sin debt of every person born of a woman in all history. God alone is the Aleph, or Ox. Jesus Christ riding a foal was to verify that he indeed he was the Son of God and equal with God as the Aleph of creation.

Jewish Kings have always ridden donkey's, not white horses. Pagan kings and pagan leaders ride white horses. Jesus Christ will not ride a white horse until he receives his kingdom at the end of the tribulation of the last seven years of human government on earth.

When Jesus Christ presented himself as the worthy lamb, the common people accepted him as their king. God killed two birds with one stone. The stone which the priest class builders rejected, was accepted by the common people as their messiah and future king in Israel. Hosanna, blessed is he who comes in the name of Yeshua ha Messiah! Hallelujah.

Nisan 10 brings us to the date of the crucifixion. Nisan 14. In Israel it is called Passover. Passover is the date Jesus Christ was crucified in Jerusalem. It has never changed. The Roman's changed the calendar to fit their pagan pantheon and bring Christians into the pagan fold. Passover is always on Nisan 14 no matter what pagan day denominational churches make it.

This is important to understand the date of the Resurrection. The resurrection always occurs on 17 Nisan. It is the day

Noah released the dove that did not return unto Noah. The Dove is the picture of the Holy Spirit in your Bible. God has never changed. Christians have, and to their own demise.

The Roman Caesar's gave us Ishtar. She is a goddess who is represented by the head of a rabbit and the body of a naked woman. It is steeped in human fertility and human sexuality. It has nothing to do with our Jewish messiah's resurrection. There is power in the resurrection, and none associated with the worship of Ishtar from whence we get the English term easter. Nothing holy about easter. You can do what is right in your own eyes to appease your children, however you have angered the creator of the universe.

He is a jealous God that is about to completely abandon America! The Roman Catholic Church named the first Sunday in spring that follows the spring full moon, after the spring equinox as easter. Every- thing about it is pagan, and God is not playing let's make a deal. If you do not want your teenager pregnant, then stop worshipping on easter.

Nimrod is alive and well in our three-dimensional houses of worship.

From Nisan 17 we travel forward 50 days and get to the Jewish feast of Pentecost. In our bible Jewish men were required to travel to Jerusalem on Pentecost to present the first-fruits of their harvest to the priests. Pentecost is the day Jesus Christ appeared to 120 Jewish disciples and anointed them with his holy spirit for the purpose of leading people to a knowledge of salvation in him alone.

These were Jewish men who came from the ends of the earth. They came speaking languages other than Hebrew. And God anointed them to preach the gospel in their native tongue. These men would be the first-fruits of salvation. They were indeed Jewish and they spoke with other tongues than Hebrew, which is the language of love in our bible. God would not do what pagans do. He would never give them a gift that did not edify the entire body of believers. No Satanic jibberish spoken at the feast of Pentecost Jesus Christ showed up on.

God is not the respecter of persons. Tongues can be biblically discerned only when a Christian takes the entire bible literally, and we lose our religious pre-suppositions. If you want to edify the body of Christ by speaking in another tongue, then try Hebrew. It is the tongue Jesus Christ witnessed to the Jews in. It is the language of the Old Testament from where we learn how to receive God's mercy.

The feast of trumpets is yet future. I believe it is tied to both the rapture of the bride of Christ, and as a warning to the body of Christ. The trumpet delivered Jericho into the hands of the Jewish people, and began their exodus from pagan religious bondage. After God won the battle of Jericho and brought the Jews into their promised land, they immediately began to compromise with the pagan culture around them. That is the state of our modern Christian experience. We have allowed for the importation of Roman foreign god's and Roman cult practices. We have allowed the government to legislate the bible out of the lives of our children for fear of martyrdom.

This phenomenon began at the church of Pergamos. Jesus Christ labeled it as the seat of Satan on earth. Our Government Model in DC is a modern picture of the Roman government in Western Turkey at the time of John's Revelation.

Zeus was born at Pergamos when babies were thrown onto fertility altars that were brass and superheated by lighting enormous fires under each one. Women brought their babies here in droves. America has done it at the convenient altar of the womb of the mother.

The denominational church being silent is to blame. Children of church goers are more concerned with Darwin's evolution than God as creator. At the heart of the matter is a government of the people, for the people, and by the people, who always move away from God under the auspices of progress.

Americans do not need God. We have an awesome military and money that can be printed forever. Blasphemy! The two golden calves must be thrown down and we must return to God to provide all of our needs according to his riches in glory.

Soon God will send Christ to retrieve his bride. This event is known as the rapture. It is the one doctrine most denominational church's refuse to teach at their own peril. Jesus Christ warned us to be ready for his return at any moment Paul wrote 2d Thessalonians because they were afraid the rapture had already occurred. The doctrine of imminence can be properly gleaned when a believer understands Jesus Christ receiving his bride at the rapture. She has been waiting patiently since his ascension for their bridegrooms return. He has been building her a mansion in the father's house for 2000 years now and counting. Are you eagerly awaiting your bridegroom to appear from Heaven and bring you home?

He warned gentile Christians not to become date setters. How-ever the Jewish pattern for keeping time has never changed. From Moon cycle to moon cycle is one month. 12 Months being one year with 360 days in each biblical year. 7 years being a shemitah cycle, with 7 shemitah's being a jubilee of 49 years. God warned Moses in Genesis 6;3 that his spirit would not always dwell with Man, for his days would be 120 Jubilee cycles.

This is the calendar Jesus Christ taught to his Jewish Apostles and Jewish Disciples. The next shemitah will fall in September in the year 2022. Do what you want with this Biblical information I intend to share my faith every day with every- one I come in contact with. I suspect the American economy will completely collapse, for God has warned us to return to our bible, and he has shown us the enemies of his message. Teshuva; repent and return to biblical literacy for the time is short.

Jesus Christ celebrated the feast of dedication while he taught in Jerusalem. For the Jews it was a holiday of remembrance for the rebuilding and rededication of the 2d Jewish Temple after the Babylonian captivity. For Jesus Christ, he was showing the Jews that their Temple was built to glorify him during the Millenial reign of 1000 years which is yet future.

The feast of Tabernacles is celebrated in Jerusalem to commemorate the Jewish wonderings in the desert after

Moses delivered them from Egyptian bondage. The bible teaches that the Jews will undergo another period of wondering in the same desert.

When the armies of anti-Christ surround Jerusalem, the Jews will once again be forced into the desert this time the desert of Jordan as God delivers them by holding them in modern Petra. Petra translates as sheepfold. When this event occurs, the entire world will be united to stop God's plan to redeem the land of Israel and the nation he birthed in Egypt. Jesus Christ returns to Jerusalem with his bride to set up his kingdom on earth forever. No more pagan world government. Where the carcases lie, there the eagles will be gathered.

The 25th of December is the celebration of the winter solstice. It has nothing to do with Christianity. The Roman Catholic Church is responsible for Christians celebrating a pagan holiday complete with pagan rituals. Beginning with the cutting down of an erez tree and decorating it with silver and Gold and topping it with an homage to Lucifer. The son of the morning is a reference to the Roman celebration on Saturnalia. The Star on top of your tree venerates Lucifer and the religion he Birthed on the banks of the Euphrates in Babylon. Nimrod was the first Pontifex Maximus, Caesar adopted the title, and now every Pope adds that moniker to their name. Read Jeremiah 10 and you will understand how God feels about the celebration of Christmas.

Martin Luther fell short in returning us to sound Hebrew hermeneutics which Jesus Christ practiced. The entire Christmas celebration is pagan. St. Nicolas is the head of the Nicaolaitan sect Jesus Christ said he hated 14 times in the

New Testament. Jeremiah 10 Vs. 1-4 lets us know how God feels about the pagan worship of the winter solstice. God asked Israel why do they do like the heathens? The Mistletoe is a pagan fertility drug used by priests to bring on fertility in women.

Not one Holiday venerated by Christians in America has anything to do with Christ. Church tradition long ago replaced thus says the Lord in our bible. Greek Eugenics has led to denominational religious thinking and the separating into pagan tribes.

I am a messianic Christian. I am a Jew who believes in Jesus. God does not give me the luxury of separating his love for me from the history of my ancestors. We were given the oracles of God, and I have a responsibility to teach them to those who would forgo tradition in favor of God's salvation.

Jesus Christ is dealing the death blow to church tradition. Laodicea has manifest. Most Christians have no need of God's word. They look good on the outside, and the church bills are all paid. Christianity was never supposed to amount to comfort in a world that does not need God.

Christian testimony should always lead to persecution. Why should American Christians escape what God has watched his bride endure for 2000 years. If comfort is your testimony, then stick with denominational thinking. If you desire to rule and reign with Christ, get under the blood, take up your cross daily, and come follow Jesus Christ and me.

He was crucified upon a cross of wood yet he created the hill upon which it stood.

How to Understand the Bible

It is the God of creation's owners' manual, and warranty deed of the physical earth, and the human's born of women.

Elohim the creator is the God of time who occupies all space. He has two immutable attributes; Mercy and Grace. These are not feeling's they are who he is!

He is the God of eternal mercies; rachamim in Hebrew. Whenever you see an im transliterated from Hebrew to English, the word is a plural noun being used to identify a singular topic. In the case of rachamim, it is used to describe the comfort God provides and the place where he begins to provide it.

It has two uses in Hebrew in our Bible. The other use never talked about is it's use to denote the womb of a mother. The place of God's eternal comfort begins in the womb of the mother. That is why abortion is murder. And why every child ever aborted in the womb of a deceived woman will enjoy God's eternal mercy, and receive a resurrection body, and serve God in heaven, after being denied the chance to choose God's grace in the flesh.

Elohim is God's creative name found in Genesis 1. It is from this name that we learn the Hebrew law of first mention. We are to understand God as Elohim and then we will understand who died on the Cross of Calvary, if we have a biblical grasp of God's creative name.

Every Hebrew word can be discerned by understanding the 3 characters of the Hebrew alphabet that make up the root of the word. The creative name of God requires three Hebrew characters: the Lamed, the He, and the Mem. By adding an Aleph to the beginning, and inserting a Yod, we get to Elohim. It is a plural noun or duality. It is the Trinity preached about, but often never grasped in A-millennial Christian churches.

It is the Ox or Burden bearer, who rules with the Ruah, or Holy Spirit, and the mem or Messiah Nagib, Jesus Christ the Son of God, and king over all the earth. His kingdom is yet future and it is his inheritance promised before the foundations of the earth were spoken into existence.

He is the stone that the builders rejected that will topple Daniel's statue of varying degrees of metal.

Jesus Christ will rule over all of the nations of the earth, and he will do it from the throne established by David in Jerusalem. God is rebuilding the tabernacle of David for Messiah to return to, and he is doing it one bible believer at a time.

To understand God as Elohim, a Christian can begin to discern who died on the cross. We all have heard about Jesus of Nazareth. Most have at one time or another sat under the preaching of your mother or father's idea of an anointed man of God. If you were born in America, attended church on Sunday, followed the Roman calendar of church tradition, then you received a message born in the indoctrination factories called American for- profit seminaries.

Every writer of the bible received salvation and their message the same way that you as an individual believer should: the word of God.

As God spoke through the Holy Spirit, men were inspired to put into writing, what is the mind of Elohim the creator. His entire plan for your life is in the bible. To discern the bible, one must receive Holy Spirit conviction which begins when a person born of a woman, explains to you the good news: that the God of creation, left His dimension of time, to enter our world created by him, to be born of a virgin Jewish woman, to experience what we experience daily: rejection, loneliness, temptation, ridicule, and eventual torture and death. And he did it all to pay the sin debt of every person born of a woman.

It happens to be the only debt that matters when you die. It is the most preposterous debt payment plan in human history, that cost God everything, and cost us nothing but our daily desire to believe.

Would you rather serve in heaven or reign in hell? You alone must answer that question, and it does not take church attendance. The church left their first love in Ephesus, and it was all downhill from there.

If not for the persecuted church at Smyrna, and the missionary church of Philadelphia, church would be completely married to government in modern Pergamos: New York. In Bed with The Thyatiran Church in Washington D.C, sitting under reformation dogma in dead churches all across America. In need of nothing but their earthly collection of possessions, and serving at the synagogue of Satan in apostate Laodicea.

Thank you, Jesus, that you have always reserved a remnant of bible believers ready to be martyred by church folk in the world!

As a believer in Yeshua ha Messiah, or in English, Jesus Christ, one must be prepared to tell others about the reason for the joy that is within you. But first you must lose all religious presuppositions and convictions. This is the pattern of John the Baptist, this continued through the Jewish apostles and disciples, it continued in Jerusalem as the church faced persecution at the hands of the religious leaders, and at the hands of Roman rulers in Judea.

Religion in any form is ungodly. Faith in God's entire plan outlined in the bible, is God's perfect will for your life. Acts 17; 11 Reminds us to become Berean Christians, and find out in the word of God if what John Burns is saying is true.

I am a sinner saved everyday by the mercy and grace of Jesus Christ. I love only what Elohim the creator loves, and he loves his creation, of which I alone as a person born of a woman, am most desired by God for eventual Sanctification, and Glorification.

Mahatma Ghandi carried a Bible with him every- where he went. He once said the greatest obstacle to Christianity in India is CHRISTIANS! I myself questioned Christianity and Roman Catholicism until God used the military to send me around the globe. 45 countries on five continents in 8 years and three months 27 days: not that I was counting.

I never went to the tourist places as a Ranger. Always some third world undeveloped country, where people really struggle to make ends meet. These are the places Christianity and its' message of salvation emanate.

America is under the abandonment wrath of God, and when nations fail, God blames the people he sent into the world to preach his bible message. Christians in America are to blame for the rise of socialism and Islamism! Our military industrial complex, carried us away from our Puritan foundations.

We serve the God of fortresses while legislating God out of our lives. Ezekiel, Jeremiah, and Isaiah warn us of the destiny of nations who dwell carelessly in the Isles serving the God of fortresses. When you see the globe from God's view in heaven, America is an ISLAND! America and Israel serve the God of fortresses while claiming to serve Elohim.

The entire Bible was written to an American and Jewish audience. We are God's catalysts for the salvation of the globe, and both nations serve the Greek cult of Mithras which has its' foundations in Egypt and Assyria.

We have usurped the bible in favor of church and synagogue traditions. Those traditions are born out of spiritual compromise. Pride comes before a fall!

Mithras is the oldest venerated created god on earth. In Hebrew it is the Aleph: the burden bearer and animal of eventual sacrifice. God's name begins with the Aleph. He is our true burden bearer that became our eventual sacrifice.

In Archaeology, the Ox or Bull shows up in every empire's pantheon of created deities. From the temple of Dendera in Egypt, to The Greek cult of Mithras who was Zeus as a bull seducing Europa, to our modern cult of Mithras on wall street with its' giant brass bull.

Everyone who ever practiced polytheism has a god represented by a beast of burden with horns. The reindeer at Christmas were given to us by the cult of the Nicaolaitan's who Jesus Christ hated.

Eloi Olam Adonai Elohim! The Lord our God is one God and he will have no other gods before Him. Yet in America, every Church tradition compromises with the word. In the beginning was the Word, and the Word was with God, and the Word was God. God gave us his word and stamped it with this is the deal, not lets' make a deal. God is hosting a cosmic drama grounded in love, not a 1970's gameshow!

It is time for the body of Christ to produce Apostolic anointing grounded in God's precepts found in both testaments of our written word: the Holy Bible. I warn Christian preachers everywhere that the God you serve desires you to return to solid Hebrew foundations rooted in mercy and found only in the stories of our Jewish believing ancestors of the Old Testament.

Mercy is Grace's foundation. God would never build his house on any other foundation than mercy and you can only get to grace by traveling through mercy's cross of Calvary. An incredible paradigm that could only be authored by Elohim himself.

The entire Gospel message is encoded throughout the entire Bible, and it takes a diligent believer with Jewish friends to unlock the secrets of God, and His creative redemptive plan for humanity.

It was the sons of Issachar who know the times and seasons as they pertain to Israel. Find out who they are, and meet one, and scripture will become alive! God has turned his attention back east, and the Jewish remnant is being regathered in Israel: the land of our nativity.

One day we will return with Jesus Christ to receive his inheritance and our rewards. The crowns promised to those believers who move past justification and on to sanctification and eventual glorification: The true bride of Christ.

When a person receives salvation, Satan musters his forces to stop you from learning God's entire plan. He uses our own naivete' to keep us in three- dimensional church bondage. Humans always choose the easy road especially in America. The one thing missing in our American experience can never be learned in college. It must be experienced.

To learn empathy. That is the purpose of missionary outreach. God desires American Christians to take the gospel away from their church to those needing salvation in Christ. Which means every-body, every-where and all the time.

Thinking that God allowed us to crucify Him so we could become his morality police force is not the message contained in the word of God. If Jesus Christ came to save the world, and not Judge the world then we should do the same as Christians.

It is Christians who judge sinners more than Christ.

It is Christians who commit sin in order to hold on to their own church doctrines and dogma. Jesus Christ died to give us freedom of choice, and government will never wash your feet! You want your loved ones to receive salvation, then do not rely on the preacher for God to reveal himself to you: they are human also, and they also sin daily.

Salvation in God's mercy and grace is a minute- by- minute transaction. If you want to become Christ-like, then become Christ-like by reading the bible and finding your life in its' pages. The greatest journey you will ever take is one decision away!

It begins by falling to your knees, and realizing all have sinned and fall short of the glory of God. We owe God a debt for the sins we commit. None of us born of a woman can pay the debt. That is why God came and died to pay it for us. Without the shedding of blood there is no remission of sin, and nothing but the blood of God's sinless lamb could suffice in settling our debt. We could never earn it, and once we accept it, we can never lose it. But you better make sure you understand what you are getting in to.

To accept Christ is to go under the yoke of his Lordship. To accept Christ is to not wrongly divide the word of truth. To accept Christ is to accept the very real possibility that you will experience persecution from within the denominational church: they have a lot of market share to lose, and a lot of money is at stake for their houses where God has never dwelt.

The modern phenomena of televangelism, has decayed church doctrines as outlined by Jesus Christ from the Old Testament. If your preacher can not lead a person to Christ from the Old Testament alone, then he is not following Jesus Christ example. Jesus Christ reminds us in Revelation 12 that we are to know not our lives until the end.

The purpose of the bible is to understand that as believers, God intended for us to never be alone again. The word of God is alive as the writer of Hebrews reminds us. If you want to not be anxious, then believe the written word of God. If you want to know how to manage finances, then study God's law of tithing to a ministry that supports his entire written revealed word. If you want to be blessed then bless the descendants of Abraham!

The Old Testament reveals who the descendants of Abraham and Sarah are. If you want peace then surrender to the prince of peace. If you need redemption then serve the redeemer of our entire creation. If you want to serve God, then surrender to the God who died to serve you. If you need Resurrection in your Christian walk then surrender to the God who raised himself from the dead. His name is Yeshua Ha Messiah, Jesus Christ, and I know my redeemer lives!

Even so come Lord Jesus Christ.

RLTW John Burns 2-23-2020.

He was crucified upon a cross of wood, yet he created the hill upon which it stood.

Who is this Jonah son of Ammitai

What world did he exist in according to God's Plan of Redemption? Why Nineveh? Where is Jonah Today?

To rightly divide the word of truth requires a holistic view of the scripture, with hindsight as our navigator. Jonah was born into a divided kingdom in Israel. His name translates as dove. He was to be the mechanism by which God brought the Holy Spirit to the fallen gentile world of Nineveh.

Nineveh was the capitol of the empire of Assyria. It is located outside the modern Iraqi city of Mosul, east of the Tigris River. Jonah Prophesied during the time of Rehoboam II. This is very important in Jewish History for it is Assyria that God eventually uses to Judge the Northern Kingdom of Israel.

Jonah's world was one of confusion from the Jewish perspective. Within two generations the kingdom that David united had fallen apart, and was divided into north and south. A paradigm which would play out in our American experience.

The nation we call America had united to throw off the yoke of British monarchial absolute rule, only to be forever divided in a civil war for Christian independence. No common American won the Civil War. The elitist political powers that controlled commerce from giant Northern banks on wall street won the American civil war.

Today they work tirelessly to overcome the bill of rights, and take our hard-fought freedoms. They hide behind the Constitution, a document that clearly states the people's intention to trust politicians with absolute power over our lives. They have tirelessly worked to take our rights while enriching themselves.

The Jewish experience during the time of Jonah is exactly what America has experienced during reconstruction. Elitist politicians hiding behind the power we Americans give them over our lives. They claim to represent us the Christian majority, while enacting laws which alienate God from our human experience.

Government in any form will never sanction the Judeo-Christian tenets found in both testaments of our Holy Bible. The ancient pattern is the pattern we have followed since Solomon uttered the words "there is nothing new under the sun. "All Is Vanity! The American experience is the Jewish experience.

We are the spiritual descendants of Elijah, Elisha, Samuel, David and Joseph. We Americans who listen for the still soft voice of God in our lives, are the gentiles grafted into the Jewish vine of antiquity. God is intimately involved in the affairs of humanity whether we believe or not. America is, mystical, modern Assyria.

Soon an Assyrian dictator from Babylon will gain influence over the affairs of unbelievers. A modern Nimrod will advance peace in the middle east only to show his true colors during the tribulation. He will unite the world under the banner of Nimrod on the banks of the Euphrates.

He will gain favor with the Roman Catholic Church, and the Government of America to unite the world under the banner of the Islamic Trinity. He will exalt himself above everything called God. And he will do it all from the United States embassy in Iraq.

What does the Bible say about the Assyrian Empire? God identifies 7 gentile super kingdoms at odds with his will for the earth and his people: Those who believe God has always provided himself as a sacrifice. His plan has never changed. He always intended to leave the confines of eternity, to enter our world of 360- day years and seven- day weeks, to die on an executioners' cross to pay our sin debt!

That is the eternal Gospel message. That the creator knew in eternity past that he would one day enter the womb of a virgin Jewish woman to pay the sin debts of every person born of a woman who will believe in his preposterous debt payment plan. Yours and my sin debt is the only debt that matters when we die. Everything else is religious tradition, instituted by man.

Man has plotted a course to build great three-dimensional houses of worship, yet God is the God of time who clearly states in his word: that he does not dwell in houses made with human hands.

Assyria was one of two ancient Kingdoms prior to Babylon, that God identifies as intimately involved in chastening his people to true worship of the creator.

The Assyrian King Tiglath-Pilesser would be the first to invade the Northern Kingdom of Israel and his son Sennacherib would complete the destruction of the capitol of Samaria and eventually take the people of the 10 Northern tribes into captivity permanently.

Sennacherib was warned not to bother Judah and especially Jerusalem. He would surround the city and, God would send one angel to kill every other Assyrian warrior in his sleep. Sennacherib abandoned the conquest never to return again. It would take the conquest of Assyria by Babylon and Nebuchadnezzar, to finish the Transgression of Israel and the 70- year Babylonian Captivity beginning with the fall of Jerusalem in 586 B.C.

Assyria would fulfill Prophecy and then disappear into History only to be reconstituted at a future date we are presently watching take place. America will be the catalyst that brings about the rise of a modern Assyrian super kingdom.

Iraq is under the influence of the American superpower of Rome II. The iron mixed with clay has reached its' zenith. The country who started out as a city on a hill is under the abandonment wrath of God, and will one day suffer the judgement of nations who worship the God of fortresses.

Syria is embroiled in a Civil War. The secular Government of Bashar al Assad is an Arab nationalist entity who wears it's Shia Islam lightly on its' sleeves. The final domino to fall will be Kurdistan: The ancient Mittani people. I firmly believe the ancient Israelites who were purveyors of Monotheism have been kept in Kurdistan to fulfill God's perfect will for his creation.

When Kurdistan Falls to the Arabs, Assyria will be reconstituted, and the eastern leg of Daniels statue of metal will rise to world power. It will produce the Assyrian Anti-Christ identified by Micah in his 5th chapter 2d verse. I believe he is alive today, and I believe Muqtada al Sadr will play an important role in his rise to prominence.

He will be accepted by the whole world as a peacemaker. After 42 months he will break all covenants with the rest of the world. His desire will be to wipe out every semblance of the worship of Elohim in God's plan. He will exalt himself above everything that is called God.

I believe Shia Islam is the catalyst for his advancement. Their Twelver Islamic tradition mirrors Christ choosing of the 12 Apostles. They believe their Mahdi is alive in occultation as I pen these words. Their leaders in Iran and Iraq and Syria will stop at nothing, to include the use of nuclear weapons to advance their agenda. America will not escape the wrath of God.

The word Assyrian transliterates as the English word "terrorists." If you know the terrorists, you know the people of the Anti-Christ. Revelation 13:18 identifies the number of the beast, and it is the number of a man. I believe that man is MuhAMMAD.

The three symbols translated by anti-nicean church fathers used Greek number values to assign the number 666. I believe they were all wrong. Islam had not risen to power.

Translation into Greek was the easy road to hoe. Now we have the lens of human history by which to discern God's entire plan, and that plan included the psycho-phantic theosophy of Islam.

The three symbols John saw in his vision were the Islamic symbols for Bism- Allah Conquer. The Third symbol, is the crossed swords of Islam present on the Flag of Modern Saudi Arabia the Shahada.

In Lebanon and Iran, Islamic Jihadist organizations wear the Shahada on their right arm and over their right eye. Just like the Bible claims they would do. It is God's permissive will that allowed Islam to rise to prominence. All because of Jewish and Christian disobedience. Jonah is our example.

He was told to do exactly what modern Christians are told to do: take the Gospel to modern Nineveh.

Ancient Nineveh was identified with the worship of Baal, Moloch, Ashtarte and all other pantheons of gods and goddess worship that had its' foundations in ancient Assyria. It all started with Nimrod and his consort Semiramis with their Son Tammuz.

These were the original "creation worshippers". They were the first to depart from the Mazzaroth as given to Adam and Enoch and us for that matter. Our ancient ancestors, before the revelation of writing, man had only the Star constellations and their decans by which to understand God's plan of redemption. It has never changed.

We know that Nimrod means to rebel. He would become the world's first dictator. He would order the building of astrological temples for the worship of the sun, the moon, and the twelve constellations of the Zodiac. Putting in motion the gradual decline of Creator worship.

But God has always been on his throne. He has always reserved a remnant of believers who would die for his message of salvation to the Assyrians. The Christian Church needs to remove themselves from the three- dimensional confines of Church, and once again become the koinonos, or called out ones, and preach to our American Nineveh.

What specifically did Nineveh need first? Mercy!!! God commanded Jonah to preach a message of mercy. He was preparing the Assyrian public to one day accept, and hide Gods' remnant. They are present in Assyria today. Jews and Christians live in protected autonomy in Kurdistan. One day the predominant population of Muslims will turn on the minority Judeo-Christian population.

America will once again listen to Baalim, and turn on the Christian population in the Middle East. Sealing the fate of America in the annals of empirical history.

We are living in a time the Bible says more about than it does the time Jesus walked the earth! The uniting of the Satanic trinity is on our American horizon. Jonah's are required to go to Ninevah: Washington D.C., and preach Mercy and Grace!

What characterized ancient Assyrian religious observances? The worship of the sun, and the moon, with the 12 constellations of the Zodiac, permeated the lives of the ancient Assyrians, and Egyptians. All of the Temples in Ancient Egypt, and Assyria, were dedicated to Astrological and Astronomical predictions.

Interestingly in the Hebrew Torah, Enoch was identified as the teacher. What was he teaching? There were no books written. Where was Enoch's classroom?

I believe it was the heavens, and the earth, which Moses reminds us were created for us to tell the times and the seasons. Moses was given the task of writing the Torah for a few basic reasons.

Egypt and Assyria were the powers influencing the world Moses grew up in. Stephen reminds us in Acts 6 that the Pharaoh that knew not Joseph was an Assyrian. The Egyptians gave us Papyrus from which Moses would have learned to read and write. It was only natural for God to use Moses as the man to first write down his plan for redemption.

From Enoch to Nimrod, men taught God's' plan of salvation by viewing the stars. Nimrod polluted God's plan, and actually began to predict events according to star worship, and the priest class was created for the worship of Nimrod as god. His Title would be Pontifex Maximus. High priest of Assyria.

His wife was elevated to high priestess, and the worship of the female deity was codified in Ashtarte from where we glean the modern term, Easter. Interestingly the Ancient Assyrians deified the bunny rabbit for its ability to produce offspring at an amazing rate.

Today, modern purveyors of Ashtarte worship, hide in Christian churches, and, in our government buildings, and advancing the promiscuity that goes along with the worship of the female deity.

Ashtarte required a steady supply of babies to be thrown onto bronze fertility altars superheated to burn the infants alive. Today they just kill the fetus in the place of Gods' Mercy the Rachamim; the womb of a mother.

Abortion is the convenient way for weak men, and promiscuous women, to commit murder as a means to escape the inconvenient nature to raise children in a Godly manner. America has catapulted a nation who once worshipped Elohim as God, into the worship of the ancient Assyrian pantheon of fertility.

From Nimrod, Semiramis and Tammuz flow all the worship of created deities. They all center on human sexuality and Infanticide. They hinge on solar anomilies and blood moons.

Our modern celebration of Christmas combines the pagan tradition of cutting down an erez tree, and decorating it with silver and gold. Jeremiah warned us in Chapter 10 that this was the practice of heathens not believers in Elohim.

Jesus Christ was born on Nisan 1 in the year 4 B.C. He would die on Passover in April of 32 A.D. He was the exact age of Isaac when Abraham through faith was able to offer him as the Akedah in Genesis 22.

Daniel 9:26 further illuminates Palm Sunday as occurring on the presentation day of the Lamb, four days before Passover. April 6 was prophesied as the 173'880th day since Artaxerxes Longimanus issued the decree to rebuild the walls and the city of Jerusalem. That occurred on March 14, 445 B.C.

Jesus Christ orchestrated the tying of a young donkey's foal to a post, to be retrieved by himself later to ride into Jerusalem on the offspring of King David's donkey. The reason the Jews cried out Hosanna, is because only Jewish Kings rode humbly on donkeys. All other kings in history ride WHITE HORSES!

One day the Assyrian will don his white horse, and convince Israel he is their friend to their own demise.

It is no coincidence the four horsemen of the apocalypse ride horse's that identify the ten toes of Daniels statue. White, Red, Black and Green! The color of every Arabic flag that has come against the covenants of God. And will one day plunge the world into Great Tribulation.

It is no coincidence that Hamas chose as it's capitol Jericho. It is the original House of The Moon God. It polluted God's calendar of keeping time through the moon phases.

It worships the phases more than the creator who put them into eternal operation.

Hebrews do everything according to God's ancient calendar revealed in the Astronomy of eternity. 12 months of days according to the Moon's phases with leap year adding two days every four years. God gave us the Bible based on the ancient Babylonian calendar of 360-day years.

Jesus Christ worshipped on every Jewish holiday and sabbath, and he will only be in the temple on the new moons, and the sabbath. The sabbath has never changed. It is Friday evening sunset to Saturday evening Sunset, and will remain that way into eternity, no matter how many religious leaders continue to worship on the Roman Catholic schedule.

If you would like to know about the woman riding the beast in revelation, then read Dave Hunt's book A Woman Rides the Beast. It will explain the path followed by ancient Assyrian worship of Nimrod into the Roman Pantheon adopted by the Catholic Church. It is the biggest compromise with thus says the Lord in History.

Roman Catholics unknowingly practice synecretism. They will go through the tribulation. The reformation denominational church is labeled a dead church by Jesus Christ in Revelation. The denominational church has forgotten that Jesus Christ separated church and state when he washed the disciples' feet.

Their thirst for temporal wealth, and power, is their reward. No heavenly blessing in their future, unless they repent, and seek resurrection power in the Holy Spirit.

They too will compromise, and venerate Roman Catholic traditions and calendar dates. Christmas, Easter, Valentines'day, all- souls' day or halloween, and all other holidays that worship government more than God. If you enjoy a day off from God's command to work, then you had better spend it witnessing of the Gospel.

I have watched the heroes in my life go off to fight protracted War on battlefields most Americans know not exist. They leave the comforts of their overindulging American lives to protect our freedom to worship the God of creation. Yet over the course of my life, our American Presidents have undermined their ability to worship God while protecting America.

Every Pagan practice has been forced on our military while they wage War against the enemies of Jehovah Elohim. YHWH.

They look to an America that allows the worship of God, and the Bible, as the tenet that governs our communities, and yet it was taken from their Children. The war waged by socialist democrats to totally separate us from our rich Judeo-Christian founding has reached the crescendo.

They attack God's will for men and women in a family unit. They attack God's will for Israel to once again control God's tithe of land to himself at creation. The Angel with the flaming sword is still positioned around Jerusalem.

Jerusalem is the center of God the Creators world. Every person ever given the task to run Jerusalem Gods' way, has failed. It will take the Messiah promised by God in the garden to return to Jerusalem, and free it from Satan's Grasp.

First, Israel must purge the land of pagan deities and dedicate the temple. To include purging the land of its Roman Catholic temples built by Constantine's Mother. The Catholic Church gave us the Holocaust with silent Christian Pulpits in European churches complicit. They are not the friend of Israel.

Ask your pastor if he supports the Psalm 83 war that is fast approaching? For the Temple to be rebuilt the conquest of the promised land must be accomplished. What Joshua started Jesus Christ will complete. The seven principal cities in the book of Judges will be liberated from the usurper Edomite Palestinians.

America was sent a Judge to remind us of the time we are living in. His name is Donald Trump. He is God's mouthpiece to call us to repentance. What did America expect after relying on art and entertainment instead of God for comfort. Did you not expect that one day an Actor would win the throne of the American Presidency?

He has read the Bible, and he is fulfilling his role of leading us toward the rapture of the Bride of Christ, and the coming Great Tribulation. He will be reelected in 2024, and like every President before him who was re-elected, he will show us his true intentions.

He has been fulfilling prophecy at an alarming rate. God has wound his alarm clock for the last time.

Repent for the Kingdom of God is Nearby!

Jesus Christ gave the Apostles a clue as to when all these things would come to pass in Matthew 24. He said where the Carcasses lie there the Eagles will gather. I am an American warrior who has studied world history.

If you begin in the Valley of Jezreel, and ride north by east you will end up in the Land of Assyria between the Tigris and Euphrates rivers in Iraq. More men have fought in pitched battles between Israel and Iraq than everywhere else on the face of the Earth combined.

Carchemish, the Granicus, Gaugemela, The Arab conquests, the Crusades, Napoleon, Iran-Iraq wars, the land has never been free of terror!

Every traditional combatant in history that has opposed Israel, has an Eagle as its national emblem. One day America will unite with the forces of Roman Catholicism, and Muhammadism, to birth an Assyrian dictator.

Our embassy in Iraq is not going anywhere under our current President, and no President in United States History has ever closed an embassy unless it was politically expedient to do it!

It cost 300 million dollars to build. We ain't going anywhere! As a Nation we are at the crossroads. The cycle in American politics and God's Shmitah will give birth to a Democrat in America hell bent on Islamifying, and paganizing our America.

The American Civil War has never ended. It is showing us that Northern Democrats succeeded in encircling the South with liberal policymakers who want to outlaw the Bible in private now that they succeeded in taking it from our children. We are at War.

The weapons we fight with are Spiritual not carnal to pull down the stronghold of Liberalism. God is a conservative. His name is Elohim. He is the creator Trinity of our Hebrew Old Testament. He is Yeshua ha Messiah that died to pay our sin Debt. He is coming back as a Lion, not a lamb, his days as a LAMB ended on the Cross.

His Kingdom is an everlasting Kingdom of Jew and Gentile believers in Christ. It is a Kingdom he was promised by God the Father in eternity past. It is a Kingdom of conscious. It was offered to every person born of a Woman.

Predestination is summed up in the question do you believe God died to pay your sin debt?

God has enemies against his will. The Bible explains who those enemies are, and who they are not. He is the God of mercy and grace, and every Biblical revelation we receive must be grounded in his entire two- edged sword, our two Testament Bible.

Nothing has changed since Assyria first united polytheism. It has migrated west and found a home on the shores of our America. We have a choice to make that will seal the fate of America as prophesied by Hosea in the Hebrew Old Testament.

The Christian Church in America is the Church of Laodicea. She was the wife of Antiochus Epiphanes. He was the Syrian Greek who ruled the Eastern leg of the Roman Empire in 168 B.C. when he led an ill- fated invasion of Egypt. On His Journey back to Kurdistan he persecuted the Jewish people, and set up the Abomination of Desolation in the Jewish Holy of Holies.

The Maccabean Revolt led Rome to install an Edomite King on the throne of Israel, and the Hebrew religious leaders capitulated, and accepted Edomite rule. The Herods would rule Israel until 70 A.D. when Rome would destroy Jerusalem, and the inhabitants of Israel were sold into slavery, and shipped throughout the Roman Empire.

One day the Edomite Palestinians will unite with Greek minded Jews in Jerusalem to accept a covenant of peace with the Assyrian Anti-Christ. America will probably broker the peace deal under a Democrat President. It will not be a Peace Deal. It will end in total warfare in the Middle East such as the world has never seen.

Nuclear Holocaust! The United States will not survive, as the America we know. God will reserve a remnant of tribulation believers that he alone knows. The last 42 months of gentile reign on earth will be characterized by total warfare, with the four horsemen of the Apocalypse spreading their pestilence, disease, and, famine.

When the Jewish remnant in Israel realizes the error in their ways, they will look upon him who they have pierced, and cry out blessed is he who comes in the name of the Lord.

Jesus Christ will fulfill Enoch's prophecy of returning with 10000 of his saints to establish his kingdom in Jerusalem in Israel for 1000 years. I am a Priest King of Jesus Christ. I am His virgin Bride, and I worship no other God than the God of creation.

He was crucified on a cross of wood yet he created the Hill upon which it stood.

Even so come Lord Jesus Christ.

RLTW John Burns 1-31-2022.

A Modern Tale of Two Cities

Jerusalem or Babylon? If you were asked to choose the life of an ancient people, which one of these cities would you choose? Is there evidence to support the antiquity of these ancient cities actually existing? This question requires an epistemological view to take hold. Pre-suppositions must be abandoned! Ignorance can no longer be afforded. Apathy is suicide! Peace or War?

My lot in life is to enjoy an obsessive-compulsive nature. I thrive in absolute chaos. Social norms have always troubled me. No matter how hard I tried to fit in, I was always somewhere else. I feel an insatiable need to keep moving. Without ever knowing the destination.

Has America begun to suffer from pre-suppositions about an American dream? Is home ownership and debt actually good for people destined to keep moving?

The only socialist thought I hold on to is the thought that as a society, we should all keep moving. Settling down has euthanized the American conscious. When we are on the road, the glass is always half full! Paying for homes for

30 years requires the glass to always be half empty. It also euthanizes us to the probability of experiencing peace.

We are unfortunately in a state of perpetual warfare. The only true peace is the peace of God which surpass-eth all human understanding. The fear of the Lord is the beginning of wisdom, knowledge of the Holy One leads to understanding. Hallelujah!

Jerusalem is the city of eternal peace. It is the place where God intends to rest for 1000 years. In our world, it is the place where Satan focuses his entire attention to thwart the will of God on earth.

In Luciferian perspective, God cast me here and made me ruler over men' affairs, I will stop at nothing to stop God's will for the city of Jerusalem. I am a frustrated rebel. However, I will never give in or never give up! My target has never changed. War against God's plan for his city of peace is my lot.

I have come to the conclusion that Jerusalem must be the garden of Eden. The tree in the midst of the garden must be the cross. And the God of creation has his tithe of land centered in Jerusalem. It is his city. No man holds a monopoly.

The simple truth is God upholds Jerusalem with his mercy alone. No need for a Prime Minister, governor or mayor. God rules Jerusalem. It will experience peace only when God returns to Jerusalem to govern men on earth from his temple and throne in Jerusalem.

The Sword will never depart from David's house. His violation of the marriage covenant and promise of God to birth the Messiah through a pure Jewish virgin and offspring of King David, was annulled when he took Uriah's wife to bed. David sinned against God and man, whom God called for his purposes and created in his image.

Uriah was David's greatest general. He was Robert E Lee's Stonewall Jackson. He would fight for David to the death, and he was a Hittite. Evidence supports Uriah's conversion to monotheism. His example would have been David. Imagine how God felt with his man on the throne, and his Holy Spirit to have convicted Uriah to fight for Elohim's will for Jerusalem.

And then David bed's his wife, and conspires to successfully Murder the greatest general David had in the Israeli Army. To add insult to injury he was a gentile convert to Monotheism! Would you threaten relationship to your creator for sexual intercourse with any non- believing woman? I no longer will.

My marriage to Christ requires my faithful behavior in my marriage covenant on earth. I am married to God's plan for Jerusalem. There, he intends to watch the successful 1000-year reign of his messiah and son be sanctified. The prince of peace will be the king of peace and righteousness on earth. The kingdom of our God will once again be the kingdom of men. Hallelujah.

Babylon is the city where men first rebelled against God's plan of redemption. Nimrod was the rebel leader, a descendent of Ham who married Semiramis. Nimrod led men away from worship of Elohim as creator and toward worship of the creation.

Before the flood, anti-deluvian teachers relied on the Mazzaroth to teach God's plan of redeeming creation. Adam would have taught Cain and Abel God's plan for humanity by looking skyward. When properly identifying the 12 constellations in their order of brightness, Adam would have taught his offspring that God intended to provide himself as a Lamb through the womb of a virgin Jewish woman.

That Lamb would crush the serpent and establish a Kingdom on Earth from his throne in the garden of God: Gethsemane. Eden is Gethsemane in Jerusalem. Lucifer has been attempting to thwart God's plan since he first convinced Adam and Eve to question God's word. He still gets us to question his word when we hold to our religious traditions which violate his Living Word.

God established the Mazzaroth as a teaching tool for men to be without excuse. Nimrod led men and women to worship the Stars more than the creator who placed them there. Semiramis committed adultery and had Nimrod killed. She claimed to be impregnated by God himself supernaturally. Her son was Tammuz 1. She gave him the title the son of God. From that heresy, America has gone the way of Nimrod. Mystery Babylon and Mother of all Harlots is our country. Babylon on the Euphrates has migrated to the Hudson River. New York is the Modern Babylon. All American rebellion can be traced to New York. It is the epi-center of all things God the creator abhors.

Babylon is always synonymous with men rebelling. Nimrod became the King of Babylon and high priest of the cult of astrology and fertility. His title was Pontifex Maximus. The same title the Pope in Rome takes. Nimrod joined church and state through his rebellion

. Hebrew was the language by which Nimrod consolidated Sin. God confounded the Hebrew language. God speaks Hebrew. It is his Love language. Today America is trying to consolidate Babylonian Mysticism through the Satanic computer Algorhythm. It is no coincidence that most social media platforms had their origins in New York college dormitories

The Men and Women who have given us social media serve at the synagogue of Satan in New York. Jews in name only. The densest population of Jews in the world, and they continue to give us Babylonian Immorality. God entrusted the Jews with his message of Salvation to the world and they have gone the way of Baalim.

They continue to work to stop God's plan for the creation. They deny Yeshua as God's messiah. They continue to support the murder of Infants in the womb. They support the deification of women which continues the pattern from Semiramis.

There is nothing new under the sun. America has produced the most diabolical political system in human history. A government of the people, for the people, and by the people, was always going to move further away from God and his messiah. Israel is worse. It is no wonder the world has consolidated the United Nations in New York, for it is the political body attacking God's plan for humanity. Fear Not!

God wins. Jesus Christ will be worshipped. Every Knee shall bow and every tongue confess Jesus Christ as the God-king in Jerusalem. Be still and know that he is God! Hallelujah.

Semiramis was the catalyst for abortion in America. She had a temple erected in Western Turkey. When the Greeks conquered Western Asia minor, they gave it a Greek name: Thyatira. As a Christian one must confront that this is one of the Church's Jesus Christ admonished in Revelation 3.

Thyatira became the middle age Church Model. Babylon emigrated from Greece to Rome. Julius Caesar took the moniker Pontifex Maximus. He consolidated the Greek and Persian Pantheon with the Egyptian worship of the Sun. He changed the times and the seasons. God's Shabbat became Sunday. Caesar became the Supreme leader of the Religion of Rome and the Government of Rome all at once.

It has nothing to do with God's will for humanity. The Catholic Church follows the model of Semiramis and Nimrod. The pattern was continued through Ahab and Jezebel. Jezebel Murdered Naboth and his family to take his property. It was the first inquisition carried out upon the Jewish People. And it was carried out by a Jewish King and his Pagan Wife. A man who once knew God and chose to forgo salvation ,for a Phoenecian princess, and head of the fertility cult euthanizing Hebrew children on the Altars of Baal and Ashtoreth.

Today, Hillary and Bill Clinton are a modern abhorration of Ahab and Jezebel. They started their career in Politics in Arkansas. Their first official act was to Murder a man over a real estate deal. Bill Clinton was Raised Southern Baptist. Hillary was Raised by socio-political rich elitists hell bent on enforcing Darwin's model for the origin of the species. She will stop at nothing to stop God's plan for Humanity. The Deification of women and infant euthanasia are her Tools. She will do anything to replace God the creator in our lives. Her Days are numbered. Bill, you better get your affairs in order. God's word outlines your future as Ahab and Jezebel. You have chosen to War against God and you have convinced America to help you. Now America is under the Abandonment wrath of our creator and your plans for Replacing God will soon be thwarted.

Wake up American Jews and Christians. The Democrats party is at War with everything your Bible believes. An inquisition upon Jews and Christians will be carried out under a rabidly anti-semitic Joe Biden administration. Socialism requires the Euthanasia of any belief in intelligent design by a Loving creator. They will outlaw God in the hopes they will continue to be viewed as the demigods of our life. Teshuva! Repent and return to sound Biblical literacy. The window is fast closing on our American life. It is time to tear down Aphrodite in New York Harbor! Lady Liberty is a hoax. The Government model of liberty requires complete lawlessness. Liberty was birthed in America through trial and tribulation not handouts. Liberty in Christ requires discipline to believe in what he did not what we do!

Joe Biden is a Babylonian Mystic! He is Thyatira, He will continue the Policies of Caesar in his desire for absolute power. He had 47 years to change America's trajectory and he has not. He is anti-semitic. He is anti-Black. We will find out soon how intolerant the party he represents really is at their foundational level. He will restore abortion everywhere and expand upon New York's desire to murder Babies outside the womb. He will promote Government as God through entitlement programs that guarantee Americans of every color will never reach their God-given potential. Blacks will be incarcerated and left behind in cities where Democrats hold majority government influence. It is all part of their eugenic plan for America. The Political Elite class is back in business in our nation's capitol, and it is time for a cultural revolution based upon God's morality.

Joe Biden had 47 years to treat Jerusalem God's way, yet he chose to be on the wrong side of every National security decision made during his lifetime. He has always backed the enemies of the God of the Bible. His latest folly, the Iran nuclear deal guaranteed America would be abandoned by Elohim the creator. To deny Israel's right to God's entire Tithe of Land is heresy. To back the House of the Moon God will bring about his swift destruction.

Jerusalem is God's city of peace. The only ruler God will recognize in Jerusalem is Yeshua ha Messiah. The Only people aloud to live in Israel are Monotheist believers in Gods' plan of redemption. That plan was always the Cross of Christ. Anything added to it will bring America's swift destruction. America is under a pandemic sent by God himself. Covid 19 is Gods' warning to people who confess a belief in him to return to sound Biblical literacy and to abandon Roman Church Traditions. Covid is the Latin word for Crown and

God always removes a Nation he Loves crown after they have had 19 years to repent. 9/11 was God's warning for America to return to his word yet we moved further away.

The Church in America has failed to preach Hebrew hermeneutics. Pestilence is labeled by God as coming from him to warn the people he loves that he is angry with their attacking all of his irrevocable covenants of the Old Testament. Israel was warned for 19 years that Nebuchadnezzar was coming to destroy the Temple and Jerusalem. Sennacherib1 had deported the Northern Pagan Kingdom to Assyria and beyond. That occurred in 605 BC. Nebuchadnezzars conquest began and ended with the destruction of Jerusalem in 586 BC. 19 years of warning and America will not fare any better. A Biden administration guarantees America will be destroyed by YHWH Elohim very soon. Teshuva! Repent and Return to Faith in the Word of God in Both Testaments. You will know where we are at in God's time clock. You will find out that what I am saying is true from behind the veil of Eternity.

Joe Biden Loves Babylon and hates Jerusalem. He Loves Rebellion and hates Gods perfect order. His party has convinced the world that they are the people that can return them to Babel on the Euphrates. He will Give the Shiites control of Iraq even after so many Americans died there. He will reinstitute the Iran deal which guarantees that Israel cannot support a Biden Presidency for Iran has vowed to Kill every one of God's covenant people. Joe Biden agrees with Iran as a matter of convenience. Just like abortion where it is convenient for a woman to not be burdened with the thought of raising a baby alone, Iran destroying Israel is looked at By

Biden and his team as Politically convenient. Once again God has the last word. Babylon on the Euphrates will be destroyed by God never to be inhabited by Men again! Israel will take the Palestinian territories and finish the conquest of Joshua! Yeshua ha Messiah will be the warrior who destroys every nation united to thwart the plans of Elohim! Including Mystery Babylon, the Mother of Harlots. A nation who once glorified the plans of God has turned to glorifying the success of men, hellbent on destroying America's Judeo-Christian foundations. Joe Biden is the latest manifestation of the High Priest of Babylon who controls Government and the Priests of the Babylonian Fertility cults rampant in My America. And the Denominational Church continues to be afraid to start a Christian Insurrection! Jesus Christ Did! Hallelujah.

Jesus Christ spent the majority of his adult life in Jerusalem. He was the rightful King and only High Priest . He spoke out against his family, the Priests of YHWH, and the Roman Government. Anyone that violated God's will for their lives Jesus Christ warned. That is my calling. I am a consummate insurrectionist. America has been hijacked by a political elite class of people. Their Goal is to get God out of our lives and install Nimrod and Semiramis to be our God's. No Thanks! I serve a God who serves Me. He entered my dimension of time to die upon a wooden Cross to resurrect me from Dead American Pagan thinking. He did not die to make me or you Good. He died to raise us to new Creative Life. Stop practicing Synecretism. Return to Both Testaments of your Bible and ask for God's eternal mercy. When you do, Grace will begin to appear in your life and God will remove the veil of religious tradition currently blinding you to Hebrew hermeneutics. Jesus Christ and every writer of your New Testament preached out of the Old Testament. They Got people saved by quoting the Prophets of Old. God's model for Christian witness plays out in the lives of the Jewish people of yesteryear.

Mercy is Grace's only foundation. God will never build the house of grace on any other Foundation or footing. The Church never replaced Israel in God's eyes. The Church Jesus Christ spoke of was always going to be the fulfillment of Judaism. No need to kill innocent Lambs: The Innocent lamb was God himself, and we all Crucified him through unbelief and sin! For those who believe, Jerusalem is your Destiny. For those who do not, Babylon is your Home. That Home will be destroyed during the tribulation that is knocking at our American door. Jesus Christ stands at the Door and knocks. Please answer and let him in. He desires peace like a river for your life. He was crucified upon a cross of wood yet he created the hill upon which it stood! His name is Yeshua Ha Messiah! He is the God-Man destined to take his throne as a Lion in the city of David. His days as a Lamb ended at Calvary. Jerusalem and it's peace should be the prayer of every Christian who claims faith in God's messiah. Hallelujah.

John Burns June 7 2021. Next year in Jerusalem!! Hallelujah.

Humble Pie

That is what is needed to understand America through the eyes of the God of the bible.

To understand America, we must understand the seven gentile super kingdoms controlled by God's enemy: Lucifer. We must try to understand their commonalities, their differences, their goals, and their motives. But first we must determine where they originated, and if there is a common thread between them all.

The cradle of civilization has often been described as existing between the Tigris and Euphrates, river valleys, and the Nile River in the south in Egypt. A common trait shared by the ancients was their position in relation to rotation of the earth. When they looked up at the night sky, they experienced the same horizons and sunsets, moonrises and moon sets. They also experienced the same set of stars night after night.

They developed methods for telling time, by how they experienced the night sky. The ancients were our first Astronomers.

Enoch of the Hebrew bible has a name that transliterates teacher. I believe he taught the message of God's redemptive plan for mankind by how he viewed the night sky. That message is one where a serpent tempted man in a garden and God had to become a lamb in the womb of a virgin woman and be crucified on a wooden cross because nothing but the death of God himself could settle the sin debt of all mankind, for Jesus Christ to inherit an earthly throne back in the garden of Eden.

I believe that garden is the garden of Gethsemane.

This is the story contained in the twelve constellations of stars we view in a northern hemisphere, and, it is not by coincidence.

In each of these places we are introduced to a race of giants: In Assyria the Annunaki , in Egypt they are referred to as the Copts of Mizraim. In Canaan they are the tribes of giants that the earth dwellers daughters are having offspring with. Stories of star people that are half human, and half animal permeate their mythologies. Where is the common thread?

The oldest temple on Earth where the twelve constellations are venerated is the temple of Dendera in Egypt. A Mosaic floorcovering showing the Hebrew Mazzaroth is depicted. In Iraq and Syria, Temples venerating cosmology and the constellations can be found everywhere.

The Ziggurats in Iraq are temples from where to view the heavens. I believe they were laid out by fallen angels who actually had a heavenly view of earth.

I believe the cosmos are the movement from chaos to order, and I believe the fallen angels are the beings that influenced the building of these ancient temples. They would have been present when God was bringing the world that then was, through the laws of entropy, to get us to a point of human habitation.

They caused the original chaos, and then watched God restore order, only for God to have to flood the earth when the Nephillim offspring became too many and too influential in moving away from monotheism to polytheism.

The Nephillim gave us the first fertility cults on earth when they began to produce male offspring with female daughters of Adam. These were the days of Noah that Jesus Christ warned us would return before his second coming; will we recognize the male offspring of fallen angels and our daughters?

Where was monotheism and the worship of the Creator, replaced by the worship of the created?

Methuselah was alive when the flood of Noah came. He was the son of Enoch. What had the teacher taught him? I believe he taught him what any father would, with only the heavens and the earth as a classroom.

I would follow the moon cycles to determine when to sow and reap a garden. I would follow the solar pattern to learn to determine times and seasons. I would teach him the creators plan for his life through the constellations of stars he experienced each night.

Methuselah would pass this on to his son Lamech, and he would in turn teach his son Noah.

Noah would hold Gods' redemptive plan for humanity close to his heart, as he witnessed to unbelievers before boarding the ark with his family. His sons would know the story of creation, and would watch their father have incredible faith in God to carry out his plan.

Noah had three sons, Shem, Ham, and Japheth. They would become the progenitors of peoples all over our earth. Their names teach us how they looked and who their offspring were from a geographic perspective.

God flooded the earth to destroy the Nephillim. Fallen angels can never be saved. Only human beings descended from Adam can be saved. Yet after the flood of Noah, the Nephillim returned. They were being worshipped by all nations in the levant after the flood of Noah.

The Ark came to rest on the Mountains of Ararat. The sons of Noah would debark from the boat and release the animals and begin to build the new civilization. Over time, their offspring would inhabit lands from Mesopotamia to Canaan to Egypt and beyond.

They traveled west from Ararat to the plains of Ur. Here the Sumerian Empire would be the first to emerge after the flood. Here is where the world's first dictator appears and his name is Nimrod. Nimrod transliterates into we will rebel. He is descended from Noah's son Ham through the Line of Cush. He led the rebellion away from monotheism and away from the worship of the creator. He was proclaimed the creator of the sun.

He married a consort in Semiramis, and she proclaimed a virgin birth, and named their son Tammuz. He was proclaimed the son of God. From these three people come the entire pantheon of fertility cults and Astrology cults ever formed.

They polluted the Mazzaroth of the book of Job, that was taught by Enoch. The Egyptians deified their Pharaonic lines, and had incestual relations to keep a pure Egyptian bloodline. They believed they were the creators of Amun or the creators of the sun.

The great sphinx is the head of a young girl, and the body of a lion. From Virgo to Leo, she watches the star constellations pass by each evening, and over the period of one year, as they change their position over Egypt in the sky.

The sphinx guards the Mazzaroth. The great pyramids align perfectly under Orions' belt, one of two constellations that are visible with the naked eye and they are inter- gravitationally dependent. Pleiades is the other. They are both mentioned by God in Job 38-39 and God says he alone can loose the bands of Orion or Pleiades.

I believe the ancient Assyrians beginning with Nimrod, and the ancient Egyptians, had been influenced by the nephillim to pollute the Mazzaroth, and apply it to their own pantheon of god's and goddesses. They were the first empires in history to build road networks, libraries for learning, and scribes for recordkeeping and tax collection, and gymnasium for entertainment of the masses.

Their religion was the center of their world, and all education, and state service in construction and military service was bound up in worshipping men and women as god's and goddesses on earth. And their god's, were the sun, the moon, and the twelve stars.

Mars became the most feared deity. Sometime in the past, around the time of Nimrod, Mars and Earth were on resonant orbits, and Mars would have had a near pass by to the Earth. It would have appeared over the horizon 70 times bigger than the moon. It would have caused gravity to not act right, and earthquakes and tidal waves would have been prevalent.

Mars was adopted by Assyria and Egypt as their God of War, and Persia, Greece, and Rome followed suit.

They adopted a god for every planet the ancient astronomers discovered in their night sky. They became prolific navigators. The gods of the heavens were their guides and sensualities led to the worship of the female deity.

The God of the bible created four things: The heavens and the earth, angels, and humans, both male and female. With humans being considered one, with equality being centered in pro-genitorship.

Male and female were distinctly different in physical form and in the nephesh or soul. Men provide, protect, procreate, with different internal wiring for solving problems in our offspring's lives. Women procreate, protect, and position their Children to learn from their male Fathers. Both parents are needed for procreation, and both are needed to successfully raise a Godly offspring.

That is why the marriage covenant between one man and one woman for life, is the first covenant in the bible and the rainbow is the eternal sign that God has not changed in how he alone views marriage.

Alternative families are not of God. God hates divorce. Divorce ruins a child's perception of a Godly world. All lawlessness is born out of compromise with God's family foundation. Sexual intercourse in any form outside of God's prescribed marriage covenant, is sin, and needs Teshuva: Repent and Return to the bible!

Marriage is God's gift to human's and the very foundation by which he is building a kingdom. Our children are very confused. I was confused by my parent's separation and father's remarriage to a woman I share no DNA with. DNA is the building block of creation. It exists on the microcosm to show that God is our creator. DNA in humans transfers through the mother. DNA determines your mental state in this life.

Being raised by people other than your biological parents, may look good on the outside, but inside, children are completely confused. Breast-feeding is where the bonds between mother and child are forged. Through breastfeeding, children receive their mother's traits. They can- not be replicated by marrying a new wife. Men need to get a backbone, and stay with their wife for life. Your child's stability is on the line!

Fertility cults in Antiquity led to the Destruction of God's Family unit in America. Darwinian evolution led to eugenic thinking in Americans. Evolution and eugenics have their foundation in ancient thinking. The Greeks introduced us to the well- born stock model. Hesiod in the 8th century B.C. and Plato in the 5th Century B.C. introduced the world to eugenics as taught in Darwinian evolutionary theory.

DNA is dealing the death blow to Darwin!

Evolution gained a foothold in our schools after the Civil War. Our country was eternally divided between believing in God as Messiah, and believing in evolution. It led to great confusion in the lives of post- civil war southern homes. Eugenics taught in northern American Ivy League schools, led to the formation of the Ku Klux Klan in post war south. By 1919 the KKK was an incredibly powerful political party, and the Democrats were behind them.

The War to eliminate Jesus Christ from the American experience had begun. Behind it was the incredibly powerful Democratic party. Nothing has changed!

The fertility Cults started in Assyria and Egypt migrated to our American shores. They had a mission to euthanize anyone who does not think like them, and they think like Plato and Hesiod. They believe that they are the best stock to rule the rest of us who have been cheated by natural selection.

God created nature: God created you, and God has a plan for your life! He is alive and he sees you as needing salvation. That is what makes us equal from the womb. We all have sinned, we all need saving, and we have the same savior who provides salvation no matter how you look!

God is concerned with the inner man and woman. We are all wired to hear God's voice. To ignore it is eternal separation and eugenic thinking. The most educated people who are elevated by eugenicist's to positions of hero worship, do not know the God of the bible.

Margaret Sangar, Lothrop Stoddard, W.E.B. Du Bois, John and Robert Kennedy, The United States Supreme court of 1963 and 1973, the entire modern Democratic establishment run by the Clinton machine, with Jezebel and Ahab Clinton leading Barak Obama in the eugenic practice of believing they were chosen to rule over the rest of us who have been cheated by natural selection. Eugenic Elitism!

Abortion is a term given to the murder of the unborn. It too has its' roots in ancient near eastern fertility cults. The Hebrews of the Old Testament were warned to stop sacrificing their children on fertility altars that were not destroyed by Joshua in the conquest of God's holy land.

The god's of Phoenecia, Egypt, Assyria, Greece, and America all require babies to be sacrificed on bronze altars superheated to receive the human sacrifices needed to fulfill their lust for blood. At the center were the cult's of Baal, and Ashtarte. Both have been repackaged for current American worship in planned parenthood and American Christian churches.

The roots of Abortion go back very far in antiquity. The Lydian's established the bronze altar at Pergamos. Zeus was said to be born from the sacrifice of human babies thrown on the altar at Pergamos. Pergamos has migrated to America, and set up shop in Washington D.C. and New York City.

Children are being taught in public school by people who have been indoctrinated to the cult of abortion. Evolution is at the heart of their perverted theosophy.

Pergamos is said by Jesus Christ to be the seat of Satan on earth. The very stones of the ancient altar of Pergamos were desired by despotic murderers throughout history. The Nazi's sent Albert Speer to purchase the stones from the government of Turkey between the world wars. Hitler built his altar at Nuremberg from the Stones of Pergamon.

Stalin brought the stones to Russia, and purged millions of undesirables from the eugenic Russian civilization. When the wall fell, and east Berlin opened back up, those stones migrated to America, and are in various museums throughout our great Judeo-Christian country. Teshuva: Repent and return to the God of the bible!

America introduced the Nazi's to our idea of evolution. Margaret Sangar was concerned that African- Americans in New York city, were reproducing at too great a rate; so, she opened our first abortion clinic in Brooklyn.

Between 1909 and 1921 92% of babies aborted in New York City were Black.

She hosted the Nazi hierarchy at her international eugenics' conferences in New York City.

Lothrop Stoddard was a Harvard educated Philosopher who was a leader in The Ku Klux Klan and devout anti-semite. Hermann Goering testified the Nazi program of euthanasia was learned from Margaret Sangar at her three International Eugenics conferences.

We contributed to the deaths of 60 million people across Europe with our silent pulpits and FDR's denial of the holocaust. Eugenics taught at ivy league schools is the foundation for the modern Democratic party and its' abortion curriculum.

At the heart of their policies is deception. They have been deceived, and it saddens me to know that Jewish people support abortion. I warn Jews in America that history tells us that when our economy falters, your property and wealth will be the first targeted for theft by the democratic party of 2020.

They are an all or nothing party when it comes to eugenic thinking, and, keeping power. They will stop at nothing to destroy American families, American Christians, and eventually American Jewish brothers and sisters.

I have lived the majority of my life confused about God's role in our lives. My time in the military traveling the earth taught me that utopia can only be achieved if God and his Messiah are your foundation. Religion made it ok for my parents to separate, religion had made me the God of my world with no room for compromise.

The religious war for my soul continues. Today the Democratic machine that sent me to kill Muslims in Somalia, after watching 19 of my friends killed on October 3, 1993, allowed for the immigration of Muslims from Somalia and gave birth to a new type of American: The moon worshipping Muslim that becomes a Congresswoman, only to openly condemn 250 plus years of American history.

Then she tells me everything wrong with my American citizenship: I paid for my citizenship by being shot three times to give her countrymen and women a chance at sovereignty, and you came here to condemn me?

The American civil war continues. Northern elitists have surrounded Southern Christian peoples with their policies of infant euthanasia.

Transgenderism and homosexuality legislated by government, and open borders with lawlessness at the corps of their governance, are the Democratic model for their eugenic minded America. Blasphemy!

America is a monotheistic society whether you like it or not, and soon the second amendment will be activated to stop the insanity of legislating Jesus Christ out of our shared American experience. The only redress of grievances for a Judeo-Christian believer in America, is his gun to protect his or her free speech on our private Christian property!

I have worked my entire life overcoming men's prejudices. Government in any form, will never have a moral compass other than the one ruled by lucifer. They will always move away from God's morality outlined in the bible!

Government exists to replace God with cult worship. At the center is the ancient worship of the OX; or in Hebrew the Aleph. The Ox is a beast of burden that provides provision and it is also an animal of sacrifice. The ox has been worshipped for a long time and continued with the administration of Donald J. Trump.

The bull market of Wall Street is Mr. Trumps' Achilles' heel. He has taken on the abortion industry, but he has unabashedly led American Christians to worship at the cult of Mithras: He is following the ancient pattern of King Jehu in Israel.

Covid-19 is God's mechanism to bring America to TESHUVA! Repent and return. Repent from believing in government money as your God, and return to sound biblical doctrines! God provides all of our needs according to his riches in glory. He is the Aleph and the Tau, the beginning and the end, the first and the last, and he owns all the precious metals that back our financial system.

And yes, we live in the Laodicean Church Age that is present at the rapture of the bride of Messiah! Hallelujah! The Trumpet will soon sound and chaos will once again rule this world without the Holy Ghost restrainer to restrain rebellion.

Christians who serve at the temple of Mithras, while attending a-millennial Churches, will be depressed to find true believers in Messiah gone!

The delusion will be poured out, only martyrdom remains for the person who puts off salvation when the tribulation begins. The time has come for judgement to begin and to begin in the house of God.

Wake up believing America! The bible is the warranty deed for your life and future. Return to bible teaching, and relinquish your religious traditions in favor of thus says the LORD!

Why do I write these words? Because I love America, and I love Americans even more. I fear the generation that defeated Hitler is fading fast. Will this generation be able to defeat an American Hitler that the Democratic establishment in D.C. brings to power? Deception is their tool and they control the media, the money, the military, and they work tirelessly to control the message of Jesus Christ with the goal of eradicating Jesus Christ from our American experience.

Jesus Christ separated Church and State when he washed the Jewish disciple's feet! Does your church wash people's feet? Does your church accept tax breaks against Jesus Christ wishes? If you pay the pastor with tithes then your church should pay taxes!

If you want an expensive military machine to continue fighting for your 1st amendment right to assemble, then come out from under tax protections and rely on God to provide what is needed for your church members.

Teshuva! Repentance and return to sound biblical wisdom that begins with the fear of the Lord and Covid 19 as the Lord's current teaching tool! The Lord chastens those he Loves.

God's purposes are single-minded, and single in complete purpose: To save sinners from their own stinking thinking. Modern professing Christian's practice synecretism at their own eternal peril.

Combining the fear of the Lord with worship of government is separation from God. Elohim is not a socialist, Lucifer is!

Choose this day whom you will serve. His name is Yeshua Ha Messiah or Jesus Christ in English. He was crucified on a Cross of wood yet he created the hill upon which it stood!

Even So come Lord Jesus Christ!

RLTW John Burns 8-4-2021.

The Tabernacle

As a Christian, I am required to question how God sees the Human experience against the backdrop of Hebrew hermeneutics. The first mention of a tabernacle has never been explained to the A-millennial church. They turn to doing what their ancestors did, and cling to Greek hermeneutics. The tabernacle of God must be rightly understood to understand the human experience.

In the beginning God created the heavens and the earth. If a Christian can grasp that statement, and believe Jesus Christ is the God of creation, then the tabernacle will be easy to discern.

And the word became flesh and tabernacled amongst us. Most Christians have read the English translation to read dwelt. How-ever a closer look at Greek hermeneutics reveals that God actually was the authorized tabernacle to dwell amongst men in Jerusalem as Jesus the Messiah Nagib.

So, if God is a Tabernacle and we are created in his image, then we also must be a tabernacle of God?

The God of creation labels himself as Elohim in Genesis 1. So, if God is Elohim, then who is Jesus Christ?

How did Transliteration from ancient Hebrew to modern English determine Elohim is the proper name of God?

Ancient Hebrew renders God's title from the root of three Hebrew characters. The Lamed, the He, and the Mem. This happens to be how to rightly identify God as one God in three distinct persons. By adding the Aleph to the beginning and the Yod to the middle we get the proper name of God. Aleph, Lamed, He Yod Mem. ELOHIM!

Elohim is known in language as a duality. In this case it is a plural noun with three persons in one distinct creator God. A duality is rightly identified when used in a sentence. Today I had all of my friends over, both of them. All and Both denote I had two friends which amounted to the total number of friends I have.

In God's case, The Aleph, Lamed, He, Yod, Mem, equal God! He is the Ox or Aleph, He is the Lamed or shepherd's staff, He is the He or Ruah which is rendered in English as the Spirit, The Yod is the open hand of God, the Mem is the water both as a destructive force and the water of refreshing.

This is how to rightly divide the Word of God using Hebrew hermeneutics. Jesus Christ said in Hebrews 10:7 in the abundance of the book it is written of me. What book was Jesus Christ referring to as the book? Dare I say the Hebrew Old Testament?

When John referred to the Word becoming flesh and tabernacling amongst us, was the tabernacle the trinity or just Jesus Christ, the son of God?

If Christians are saved by the death of Jesus Christ on the cross, then, was it God on that cross? Was it God, who tabernacled amongst us? I believe it was God the creator on that Cross!

I believe when a Christian submits to the Fact that in the beginning was the Word and the Word was with God and the Word was God, then Jesus Christ was the Word who became flesh.

He was the Word who left eternity to enter our dimension of time to die to pay our sin debt!

This revelation is what leads to revelation. This is why the veil of the earthly tabernacle was rent in two.

When God gave up the Ghost on Calvary, he did it because he was veiling the gentile bride of Christ. No need for an earthly tabernacle of any sort. With the resurrection, God intended to once again tabernacle amongst men through his Holy Spirit. If, they would accept his entire testimony about who it was who died on the cross of Calvary.

Man created in God's image is a triune image. Solomon in the book of Proverbs instructs men to intreat wisdom, knowledge, and understanding. If God is a trinity, then the human condition is that we also are a triune being.

But how? The Greek translators of the Septuagent under Pharaoah Ptolemy give us a glimpse into the mind of Elohim the creator.

Humans are a Spirit, that possess a soul, that occupy a body. To access the trinity of God, one must recognize that this is a spiritual incursion behind the veil of creation. It is available to all who accept Jesus Christ own testimony as to his identity as the creator of Genesis 1.

Jesus Christ is the I am of John 8:58. He is YHWH on the cross as identified by Pilate himself. To rightly identify the sacrificial Lamb as God himself, one must understand that God is the God who promised Abraham he is the God who would one day provide himself as the lamb.

John the Baptist identified Jesus Christ as the lamb promised to Abraham as Isaac's replacement.

It is God the trinity whom we access through our spirit in communion with God's Spirit.

The Soul is the seat of reasoning in humans. It is where we learn and process experiences. It is our soul where we wrestle with principalities and powers of the air. The seat of reasoning can only be overcome with access to the Holy Spirit.

The Soul is where we become double minded. Serving the world while claiming to know Yeshua. Without the spirit, the soul is where we reason our coming actions in the flesh. If our soul acts upon reason alone, then all the thoughts of man are only evil continually.

The acts of the Flesh become the actions of our soul alone, and God is nowhere in our lives. Our flesh becomes something God can- not use.

To be Christian, not just talk Christian, requires we recognize we are sanctified through the washing and cleansing of

The Tabernacle

God's word. The Bible is the word that was in the beginning, and that every letter is written of Jesus Christ. To know the Word is to really know God.

To know God, is to surrender to Jesus Christ as Lord. To be overcomers who accept God's dowry of his own death to win our hand in Levirite marriage. Hallelujah!

Humans' have always required three- dimensional spaces in which to fellowship with God. God has always desired fellowship with men in the tabernacle he alone created without the hands of men. It is the human condition.

We were created to be the place God occupies. We are the only authorized earthly tabernacle that God will inhabit. He does not dwell in houses made with human hands. He is the God of time, who occupies all space. To be inhabited by God one must accept the most preposterous debt payment plan in human history. You can achieve this and never step foot in an earthly tabernacle! Hallelujah!

Jesus Christ died to start a kingdom, not a bunch of heretical denominational churches. His desire is that you will hear him knocking at the door of your earthly tabernacle and let him in, because the church continues to gather inside, and he is outside knocking to get in to church. He is not in church. They married the world and divorced God.

It started in Egypt. After God delivered them from the bondage of slavery, and the influence of Egypt's god's, they wondered into the desert full of the treasures of Egypt, along with the trappings of Egyptian life.

As Moses was called up the mountain to receive the law, the new nation that God had delivered from bondage, returned to the Egyptian pantheon and crafted a golden calf.

The golden calf is representative of their own financial stability. They left Egypt with treasure, God had destroyed Egypt's military in the Red Sea, and now Israel wanted to return to worshipping Egypt's God's.

This is America's story. A nation that once worshipped God, created a government of the people, for the people, and by the people, then legislated him out of their lives, and is marching toward the total abolition of God from our children's thought's.

America has created two golden calves after the pattern of Jeroboam.

Over -dependence on the bull of Wall Street and the golden calf of Washington D.C. will be our nation's death. And it is on our near horizon. America is under the abandonment wrath of God! Teshuva!

The Golden calf erected by the Hebrews in the wilderness was a direct mocking of God. The Hebrews understood that God gave them their alphabet and God was to be understood from the perspective of him being their heavenly father.

God the father is indicative of the father's identity. He is the Aleph and the Lamed identified as EL. He is the Ox and the Ox goad. The erection of the Golden calf was consistent with all religions moving from worship of the creator toward worship of his creation.

America has the religion of the Bull of Wallstreet continuing the rebellion begun in Babylon by Nimrod.

Marry that to a little bit of English Jesus, and you have the modern, amillennial Christian church. They continue to build lavish tabernacles, while God stands at the door knocking, wanting back into their salvation experience. Pergamos is on full display.

The Greek temple of Pergamos was where John identified the marriage of the church to the world system. Per and Gamos make up the Greek word meaning unholy marriage.

Jesus Christ revealed to John, that church history would follow a distinct pattern in their march away from sound Hebrew Old Testament teaching. The Church moved toward a Greek Eugenic model.

The priest class was born with bishops becoming overlords. The monopoly of mother church was born at Pergamos.

The doctrine of deifying the feminine gender was born again at Pergamos. The temple of Pergamos is indicative of every church erected in America. It receives tax breaks from the state and federal government.

If the church rendered unto Caesar what belongs unto Caesar, every citizen in America would see their tax burden decrease. And the church would actually begin doing something Jesus said.

More people would listen to the message of Christ if the church would quit looking exactly like the world around them. Complete with a business plan, they corrupt God's seedtime and harvest message.

They receive incredible amounts of money from willing gamblers who actually believe that planting a seed of money will guarantee a bigger harvest of money. How does that fare with Christ teaching, to not store up for yourself treasures on Earth, but store up for yourselves treasures in heaven.

The Gospel was freely given by Christ himself. Planting the seeds of the Gospel has nothing to do with collecting money in lavish tabernacles. The seeds you should all be planting is the reason for the joy that is within you.

His name had better be Yeshua Ha Messiah. He had better be understood as God incarnate and eternal. You better believe he died to pay your sin debt. You better begin reading his entire word to prepare for the coming kingdom promised to Jesus Christ in eternity past.

That kingdom will be governed in the millennial temple in Jerusalem. That is the only temple we as Christians should support. Israel is on a collision course of destiny. They will begin the building of the temple in the city of David. Setting in motion the final seven Years of Human Government on Earth.

The Rapture will be in the rearview mirror of the bride of Christ. The wedding of believer with our heavenly bridegroom will occur after Jesus returns to receive his reward, the bride of Christ.

The Tabernacle

The Body of Christ, will see some go through the tribulation. But take heart, you can still be martyred and enter heaven at the second resurrection. Now is the hour of salvation.

The Bible subject that takes up the second most scripture happens to be the description of the tabernacle. Only the subject of Christ occupies more space in scripture. The tabernacle is the Christ and Christ is the tabernacle.

Spirit, soul, and body. Wisdom, knowledge, understanding. Father, Son, and Spirit.

Are all synonymous with the tabernacle and its' architecture. The human condition is addressed by every aspect of the temple layout. The outer court, the holy place, and the holy of holies all point to our total dependence upon the word of God to understand our relationship to him.

Justification by faith in the Word of God is our first step. Faith birthing sanctification and dependence upon God's word for all questions regarding how to rightly divide the word of truth, comes second in our faith walk.

Sanctification will lead to our eventual glorification in Christ coming kingdom.

The Christian destiny is for Christ to occupy our earthly temple. He desires to inhabit your Spirit, Soul, and Body. Will you answer the still soft voice of God? Will you become the habitation of Christ who became flesh and tabernacled amongst us?

You can become the tabernacle of God's Holy Spirit. Listen for God's whisper and say yes Lord, I believe you died to pay my sin debt! Hallelujah.

The overdependence of Christians upon three -dimensional spaces has isolated sinners outside of your denominational theatre. The tabernacles bearing the symbol of the cross on their facades, long ago stopped preaching the blood of the lamb alone can cleanse a sinner of his sin.

That Lamb was God himself. The alternate gospel being perverted in cults of every sort in America, will collapse, and God will return us to the Acts of the Apostles.

The Message of the Lamb is being taught in houses once again. Families should take advantage of the current pandemic and repent and return your family to sound biblical literacy. God needs your children bible trained to enter the world.

The world is where the sinners God desires in the kingdom exist, and your children are needed to witness of the message of Christ. Taking the name of the Lord in vain has nothing to do with vocabulary. It is all about being an ambassador for Jesus Christ to a fallen world.

While we build elaborate churches with competing doctrines, God has been building a kingdom one testimony of salvation in the blood of the lamb at a time.

He is God and he can get his message to his creation without ever stepping foot in a denominational church. The tabernacle of God is the body of a true believer. He occupies all the thoughts of his children, and they in turn recognize their responsibility as the virgin bride of Christ.

We are approaching a period of time when the Apostate church will be on full display. They have no need of the blood of the lamb, because they have amassed incredible earthly wealth, and Jesus Christ says they have their reward.

To become the tabernacle of God's Holy Spirit, one must allow God to crucify your members. The first domino to fall should be all of your religious pre-suppositions. The Bible alone must become your pastor. God is capable of ordering your foot steps and he is more than capable of getting you the message from the bible he alone crafted in eternity past. Mercy and Grace await. Whenever mercy is exhausted in the lives of God's people, grace appears! Hallelujah.

The tabernacle of David is the only tabernacle God says he will raise up. David's tabernacle was the tent of meeting he carried from the house of Obed-Edom to Jerusalem. It housed the ark of the covenant. Within the ark was Moses staff that budded almonds. Almonds are indicative of two harvest in a season.

It was signifying how God would harvest his creation, and Israel at two distinct periods of time. The first-fruits were harvested at the resurrection, and the second harvest will be at Christ second coming at the end of the 7- year- tribulation.

The Tabernacle of David offered unfettered access to God. The sides of the tent were rolled up, and Israel had 24/7 access to YHWH and the shekinah glory of God inhabited the mercy seat.

That is the pattern of redemption.

The final temple will see unfettered access to the mercy seat in Jerusalem. Christ will be ruling and reigning with his bride, and David will be present to receive his inheritance as the first-fruits of resurrection. The tabernacle of David will be established forever, and Jesus Christ will be worshipped for all eternity as the King of the Jews!

Understanding that you were created to be the tabernacle of God has never been more important.

Teshuva is required of everyone who believes Jesus Christ died to pay their sin debt. Teshuva means repent and return to sound Bible literacy, your rewards and inheritance in the kingdom of God require it.

Do not believe me believe God.

Study to show yourself approved, a workman rightly dividing the word of truth. God's Bible is the only word of truth that exists. It is a Love Story written by the creator of the universe. The central plot is the redemption of creation which Lucifer corrupted.

The central players are us as the sinners and Jesus Christ as the Messiah who is sinless. At the heart of the matter is your salvation. If you were the only sinner, Christ would have still died for you! Hallelujah.

It is time to sanctify the tabernacle of God so he can inhabit our entire being. It begins with biblical humility in realizing we all like sheep have gone astray. We are all in need of God's Mercy and Grace.

We all need to return to God's Bible for all matters of morality.

Pray for God to make you the tabernacle of God. He will inhabit you, and keep you from the hour of temptation.

He was crucified upon a Cross of wood, Yet He created the hill upon which it stood.

He is the Aleph and The Tau. He is coming soon to rapture his bride. Will you be watching for his imminent return?

Even so come Lord Jesus Christ.

RLTW John Burns 6-21-2020.

The Architecture of Ruth

The opening of the Book of Ruth is the most theologically rich first line in any book of the Bible to eclipse Genesis 1;1. To digest Ruth 1;1 is a lifetime of time spent behind the veil of eternity.

The story begins in the time of the Judges, with a Jewish family of the tribe of Judah, enduring a famine in the land, God had promised, would be a land, flowing with milk and honey. Jacob had anointed Judah to be the patriarch of the coming Messiah King. Elimelech and Naomi are the key players in the cosmic love drama orchestrated by none other than Elohim himself.

Joshua had failed God in not cleansing the land of the polytheistic Canaanites, who occupied the land that God intended to sanctify to himself alone. It may be hard to stomach some hard truths about the God that people claim to be Lord over their life, they can- not understand that he will allow famine and pestilence to chasten his creation to obedience to his perfect will.

It was never intended to be Christ crucified to make bad men good. Christ died to raise dead men to life! Dead thinking about what God intended for his creation, permeates the Christian denominational Church's mindset, just as Jesus Christ told John would happen. Revelation 3 addresses the church of Sardis. It is the reformation dead church that followed the middle age church of Thyatira, The Catholic Church which has persecuted true believers in the Bible since 323 AD.

Jesus Christ said Sardis was dead and in need of resurrection. Sardis is the reformation started by Martin Luther. It led to the formation of eugenic Christian denominations of all flavors. No unity in the body of Christ here. My way or the highway Christianity. We better get back to God's way. Teshuva is needed. Repent and return to God's will found only in the pages of the Bible. Church attendance can- not pay your sin debt. Only time spent with Christ in his written word can sanctify and glorify a justified believer. It is the book of Ruth where God annunciates his perfect will for creation.

Elimelech is the patriarch of the narrative. His name is loaded with clues as to what God's will is for his life. The etymology of the name can be traced to Hebrew-Chaldee in the Lexicon. Aleph ,Lamed, Yod, Mem ,Lamed, and Waw. The six Hebrew characters tell us a great deal about this man.

The Aleph is representative of the burden bearer who would also be a sacrifice. The Aleph is the OX. It is the first letter in the name of the God of creation, our trinity. The Lamed is the shepherd's staff or crook. It has two ends. It is indicative of the divine attributes God alone possesses: Mercy and Grace. It is also indicative of the two- edged sword of the

Bible. The Old and New Testaments are one sword with two edges.

The Old Testament is the story of mercy found in the lives of our Jewish ancestors. The New Testament is the arrival of grace in the person of Christ. When mercy had been exhausted, God appeared in the womb of a virgin Jewish girl to pay the sin debt of all humanity. He also announced his intentions to reunite Jew and Gentile through the cross.

The Yod connects the Ox and the shepherds' staff with the Mem. The Yod is the smallest Hebrew character, yet it is the open hand of God to his creation. It is the open hand of correction and the open hand of blessing. To connect the burden bearer with the shepherd with an open- hand leads to the Mem.

The Mem is indicative of Water from a fountain. It is the Waters of the Jordan that reconnect the Levites of the priest class with the king from the tribe of Judah. It is the waters of Lucifer's flood in Genesis 1;2 that brings about the creation of our world made habitable exclusively for human's.

Our world was uniquely created by Elohim for the purpose of discovery. It was taken from the flood waters of chaos brought about by Lucifer's rebellion.

Everything we know about our creation is post Noahic flood. Science will be stymied by unbelief, until they begin to accept God's creation narrative from a Hebrew hermeneutical perspective. Science will linger in abstract theory, and deny evidence to complete the transgression.

Hydrogen and Oxygen were created by God to allow us to understand that his waters never recede and never run out. For the cleansing of the flesh and the spirit and soul. This is the Mem of Elimelech. The waters that connect God and Jesus with the creative intention to unite Jew and Gentile through the second Lamed and the Waw. The second Lamed in the name of our patriarch is indicative of Jesus Christ the shepherd to the gentile bride. God the father is Israel's eternal shepherd, and Jesus Christ is the Good Shepherd of anyone who would believe in this preposterous debt payment plan.

Jesus Christ and, God the Father, alone possess Mercy and Grace. Hallelujah!

The Lamed leads to the Waw. The Waw are the nails that made it all possible. The three iron nails that nailed God to the tree in the garden of Eden. He did it all because he loved you. Elimelech is how God began to illustrate his plan for Israel and all creation.

The famine would lead to Elimelech taking his Jewish bride to the gentile world. To save the remnant.

God will go to extreme measures to chasten his creation to hard truth. Naomi is indicative of Israel. The bride of God the father. God hates divorce, so he will not leave Israel disconnected from her inheritance. We are watching God fulfill Israel's destiny, and it began in the book of Ruth.

Israel as a nation will endure the seven worst years of persecution she has ever endured.

She will be washed and cleansed by God alone. This event occurs when Israel is at peace and in the land. It is the Last seven years of gentile government on earth. We are on the cusp of God winding his Jewish timepiece for the last time.

Jesus Christ warned his bride to be not deceived. Biblical illiteracy has led Church's to follow church tradition more than believe the entire word of God. Replacement theology denies God's plan for Israel and Jesus Christ. To deny God is saving the Jewish people is akin to calling God a Liar.

How has that worked out for Lucifer and one-third of the angels? For Naomi to fulfill her God given destiny of saving the Jewish remnant, she had to be exiled from the land. So off to Moab they traveled. Soon after arrival, her husband and provider Died. A woman in a man's world. She had no chance. Her sons married outside the Jewish family and took gentile brides. Orpah and Ruth are the two gentile brides. One an incredible unbeliever, and one an incredible believer.

Orpah is a derivative of four Hebrew characters. Ayin, Resh, Pe, and He. Orpah is indicative of the gentile bride that looks away from the Spirit of God toward Church tradition. Ayin is the Eye. Both outward expression and inward revelation. God does not view our existence the way men see it, especially in church. Orpah went to church rather than turn to the inward spirit. She relied on the word of Naomi rather than the word of God.

The ayin takes us to the Resh which indicates she is the first gentile bride to look away. The Pe indicates she looked to the serpent, and gods of her ancestors, rather than believe what Elimelech would have professed about the blood of the lamb cleansing us from all unrighteousness. Just like Eve, she trusted the serpent more than she trusted the word of God.

The He is the Spirit of God. This indicates God's desire to give us his spirit and so often we stick to what we have always done. Going to church to try to pay our own sin debt. Judging others, rather than looking in the mirror of the word of God to see if what John Burns is saying were true. Orpah is a sad allegory and paradigm to what has happened to the Christian church in America. Church tradition over thus says the Lord. Blasphemy!

Orpah leads us to our heroine. A real woman of Elohim. A monotheist in a polytheistic world. Ruth is the most important woman in world history. Like Rahab her great grandmother, God saves the Jewish remnant through a gentile woman. Thus, allowing our Messiah to fulfill God's perfect will for his life. Ruth has a name in Hebrew that translates as friendship. She is the friend of Naomi, as the Church was always intended to be the Friend of National Israel.

Her name is gleaned from three Hebrew characters. The Resh, Tau and He. She is indicative of the first gentile bride through which God intends to save his people, by the cross and by the power of his Holy Spirit. Resh is the first. The Tau is the Cross of Christ, The He is the Holy Spirit of God. Hallelujah! Ruth is the allegory God uses to show us he always intended to save creation by allowing himself to be crucified upon the cross. Of the Jew first and then the Greek!

He would then allow the Holy Spirit to spend the next two thousand years and counting, to convict people of his plan. Grace came By Jesus Christ through the Holy Spirit. Jesus Christ ascension after his resurrection continued the paradigm of God exiled from his bride, but through Christ death, The Holy Spirit is given to all who would believe. Jesus Christ is in heaven building our mansion. His inheritance is to rule and reign over Israel from Jerusalem for one thousand years. It is a future event that was revealed to us through John the Revelator and the Old Testament prophets.

Jesus Christ himself in Matthew 23 tells us the tragedy and triumph of God over his creation. The Jews knew not the hour of their visitation. God allowed them to be exiled from the land after they denied Christ. It is However God's intention, to again bring Israel into the land to chasten them to belief in Yeshua.

One day they will cry hosannah, blessed is Yeshua who comes in the name of the Lord, but only after looking upon him whom they have pierced, and acknowledging Jesus Christ as their king and priest forever! Ruth began the paradigm.

We must address the names of the sons of Naomi. Mahlon and Chilion.

Mahlon translates as sick. He is the diagnosis God has placed on Israel at the time of the judges. They wanted the blessing's of YHWH Elohim, however, they were not willing to carry out God's word to the letter. They allowed polytheism to permeate every aspect of their existence.

They refused to kill the enemies of God in his tithe of land at creation. The enemies of God's plan had an alternate morality that revolved around the sacrifice of children upon fertility altars. Israel had begun to believe more in their military, then in trusting God. They had become incredibly wealthy when leaving Egypt. Their wealth was more important than their relationship to God as creator. America is modern day Mahlon.

God hated that Israel signed treaties with Godless neighbors. We are living in the time where America has legislated God out of our lives and we will suffer the fate of Sodom and Gomorrah. America, Like Mahlon, is under the abandonment wrath of God. Teshuva! Repent and return to the word of God.

Mahlon is made of 5 Hebrew Characters. Mem, Keth, Lamed, Waw, Zayin. The Mem is the waters of judgement found in Noah's flood. Mahlon is the church judged. The Kheth is representative of an enclosed or fenced area. Mahlon had a fence erected around him that he could not escape. He married outside the Jewish family thus eliminating him from being the father of Messiah. He fenced himself in.

But God has mercy that is everlasting. The Lamed denotes God's intention to always be the good shepherd. He has only two divine attributes: Mercy and Grace. His shepherd's staff indicates he shepherds the same way from eternity past as he does today.

The Waw is indicative of the only way man can return to God. The Nails. You must nail your past to the cross of eternity. Zayin is indicative that Mahlon was not willing to be chastened, so sickness was his lot unto physical death. Zayin represents the sword of the Lord which is the word of God.

God uses the same sword he used in the garden that he uses today. It is the two-edged sword of our Bible. Every letter, every word, every punctuation mark. It is all from God and none can be added or taken away or God becomes a liar and that is impossible! Hallelujah!

Chilion. His name translates as "Pining". Constantly complaining. This is the disease of the modern Christian church.

It is a veiled reference to the nation of Israel. His name can be gleaned from five Hebrew characters. Qoph, Lamed, Yod, Waw, Zayin. The Qoph is the nap of the neck or the back of the head. It is indicative of God's mercy and grace upon Chilion's life. God had carried him into Moab, and away from the famine in Israel. He had found him a gentile bride of God's choosing. Yet he complained constantly.

The Lamed indicates it was always God who was shepherding Chilion. God extended the open hand of blessing to Chilion in the Yod, while chastening him through human sickness. God would chasten him and The Waw is indicative of God's intention of saving Chilion through the nails of Calvary. God intended to nail Chilion and his complaining to the Cross of eternity. The sword of Zayin, indicates that judgement was Chilion's lot. It all occurred while he was exiled from Israel.

The Architecture of Ruth

That is God's intention for apostate Israel and the apostate Christian church. Mahlon and Chilion are indicative of what is coming upon the Jews of the diaspora who have not returned to Israel, and the Christians who will not allow themselves to be chastened to the word of God alone.

Church tradition has replaced thus says the Lord, and the church has been completely deceived. Teshuva! Repent and return to the Word of God!

Naomi is indicative of the Nation of Israel. Ruth is indicative of the gentile bride Jesus Christ alone will marry. She is a virgin bride, cleansed in the blood of the lamb taken from the waters of judgement. Naomi's name translates as the almond tree. The almond tree can produce two harvests in one lunar year. Naomi is indicative of God's desire to redeem Israel a second time. First out of Egypt and second out of the revised Roman empire.

In Both cases Israel was exiled from the land until God supernaturally stepped in, and brought them back into the land. The exile to Babylon was the continuance of the pattern. The judgement of Babylon in the book of Daniel, was to forgive the transgression of not keeping the Shemitah for 490 years. 70 years was Israel in Babylon after the conquest of Nebuchadnezzar in 586 B.C.

The first-fruits of Naomi's exile, were the resurrected believers who visited Jerusalem at Jesus Christ resurrection. They wondered the streets of Jerusalem for fifty days witnessing of the resurrection. How many of us witness of our resurrection from dead church thinking? The blood of the lamb is the only thing that can save us from sin!

Naomi has a name that is gleaned from four Hebrew characters. Nun, Ayin, Yod, and Mem. The Nun is representative of a fish. It was the Nun that was the symbol of the first century church. It denotes God's intention to be a fisher of Jewish and Gentile believers from eternity past. The Ayin is indicative of God's eyes. He will never leave us nor forsake us. He took Naomi into Moab to save her from famine. God delivers a believer from their past, knowing his spirit will redeem their future. We then become fish captured by God's open hand. The Yod. The hand of correction and the hand of blessing. The mercy and grace of God, given freely through the Holy Spirit.

The trinity was united when Jesus Christ left the waters of Jordan. Baptism means nothing if we never leave the water and enter the Spirit! It was Naomi who first asked Orpah and Ruth to return to their pagan ancestors. Jesus Christ told us that in the last days there would be Jews who were Jews in name only. They would serve at the synagogue of Satan. They are the Jewish remnant who refuse to acknowledge Jesus Christ as Messiah and King. They control commerce and the world's monetary system. In America they control the Democratic party.

They serve at the modern temple of Pergamos in Washington DC. Aphrodite adorns their pagan temple on capitol hill. They legislate the murder of the unborn, and they support socialism, which inherently denies the existence of God as creator. They have assimilated with pagan society and they are comfortable in their immense wealth.

They have no need of God the creator or his two-edged sword. They have brought the abandonment wrath of God upon America by denying that God anointed them to carry the word of God to a fallen world. I am one of those Jews! I slumber no longer. Next Year in Jerusalem is my prayer.

Ruth went with the Spirit of God in her inner being. She returned to the land of Naomi's nativity. Bethlehem. Luz: The land of the almond tree, and, where I believe the garden of Eden has always been.

Naomi translates as my delight. God's delight has always been in the almond tree of the nation of Israel. He has not always delighted in the affairs of his people! The Book of Revelation tells us that two-thirds of Jewish people worldwide will not survive the coming great tribulation. Far more than who died in the Holocaust. Bethlehem is where God has always intended to establish his covenant on earth.

It was at Bethel that Jacob built the altar to sanctify the land. Bethel can be gleaned from three Hebrew characters. The Beit, Aleph, and the Lamed. Bethlehem is gleaned by adding a He and the Mem.

The Beit is the house. The Aleph is indicative of the burden bearer of the house. The Lamed is the shepherds' staff or crook. Bethel is the place where God established his house forever on earth.

Mercy and Grace were birthed at Bethlehem. God added the spirit and the water to the house at the birth of Jesus Christ in Bethlehem. It is a supernatural place on Earth.

Jesus Christ was born in Bethlehem. Today, 2000 years later, lambs bound for the temple sacrifice are still born each year in Bethlehem. It is under the control of the Edomites whom God hates, and the book of Ruth highlights that one day, Bethlehem would be under the authority of antichrist.

Bethel is one of the principal cities where Joshua failed to put every man, woman, and child to the sword. It was a supernatural war between God and the Nephilim, and Joshua failed to cleanse the land of the pagan's who welcomed impure offspring. Today the Palestinians control the land of Christ's nativity. But God will win in the End! Hallelujah.

Moab was the land where God brought Elimelech and his family. It is the land of the descendants of Lot, through an incestuous relationship marred with gentile deception. Ruth is the direct descendant of Lot, Abraham's nephew and his eldest daughter.

Her name is not mentioned in the Bible. Her mother has been turned to a pillar of salt. Her husband has died due to unbelief, when warned by their father to prepare to flee. Homosexuality was the lot in Sodom and Gomorrah.

They Legislated God out of their lives, they did not recognize the angelic messengers, they denied the word of God sent through their father. Sounds Just like church in America to me. God commanded Lot to grab his wife, His daughters, and escape. It took Angels grabbing them by the hand to get them to leave the world they had come to love more than God.

Momma looked back. She had become as useless as a pillar of salt. Lot makes his way to the mountains of Zoar, where his daughters get him drunk on wine, seduce him, and have his babies. Lot is a gentile. He is saved from Sodom and Gomorrah because of the word God gave Abraham his uncle. His land is where God intended to save his people through gentile Ruth born in Moab. Only God could orchestrate this love story. Hallelujah,

God's mercy is on display despite the paganism his beloved practiced while professing to love him with their mouth. God saving gentile's throughout history, through the nation of Israel and the sacrifice of God's lamb on Calvary.

Lot's son became the progenitor of the Moabites. They occupy the land of Jordan along with Edom and Ammon. Ammon is the brother born to Lots youngest daughter and he is the progenitor of the Ammonites. They too survive the great tribulation, and are today present in Jordan. The Arab's call them Palestinians.

I believe God will one day save these people as they turn to Jesus Christ for salvation once the Assyrian Anti-Christ unites the Satanic trinity of Pope, Mahdi, and a psychophant that exalts himself above everything that is called God. He is a leader out of the western leg of the Roman Empire, you will recognize him as he governs through lawlessness.

Where the carcasses lie, there the Eagles will be gathered. This is Jesus Christ warning us, of who would one day completely turn on Israel and God's plan of redemption.

Every nation that flies an eagle on their banner, will turn on national Israel. America will one day soon elect an Antisemitic president who persecutes the Jewish people in

America, to seize their wealth after he collapses the United States economy.

The Cult of Mithras in America will be judged by God himself. It will cause the United States to attack Israel. The Carcasses lie in the valley of Jezreel. Tell me another place in world History where more soldiers have died!

Jesus Christ looked across the Valley of Armageddon toward Mt. Carmel from his home in the Judean hills of Nazareth. As a little boy he dreamed of coming back a second time to unite the entire world under God for the last time. The Oldest prophecy in the Bible is Enoch seeing Jesus Christ coming with ten thousand of his saints, to destroy the enemies of God and Israel.

And Jesus Christ dreamed of his second coming!

To think, God orchestrated the crucifixion of his own son, The burial of Judaism in the garden tomb, no need for any more innocent lambs to die. We killed the one that mattered to all creation! But he rose again three days later to raise us all from dead thinking about God and who he is.

God would begin the resurrection of national Israel, in Moab. Ruth was his gentile bride prepared by the spirit of God. Naomi was the Jewish catalyst through which God has orchestrated it all. For better or, for worse, it has been Gods' perfect, permissive will, all along. Now he needed a kinsman redeemer to redeem Chilion, through a gentile bride chosen by God. While Chilion complained, God prepared his wife to meet her redeemer: Boaz. He is the hero of our story, co-ruling with Ruth in the end.

This is the inheritance of the true virgin bride of Christ who have not committed adultery with government as God on earth. The Church married the world at Pergamos. Boaz and Jesus Christ are your only hope. Whether my Jewish brothers and sisters are willing to admit it, we have been complaining about God's Messiah since we denied him on Palm Sunday in32 AD. Four Days before we crucified him, we denied him as our kinsman-redeemer. The last two thousand years are leading to our eventual chastening as we have never been chastened before. As a person who had a Jewish mother and a Roman Catholic father, No one was more confused about God. I am no longer confused.

Jesus Christ has always been God's single vision for every person born of a woman.

Boaz is a picture of messiah woven into the biblical narrative. He is introduced as the kinsman redeemer. He is the near kinsman to Elimemech, and he lives in Bethlehem. He can redeem Ruth and Naomi but only after a closer kinsman to Naomi denies his birthright.

Jacob and Esau are a continuation of the biblical paradigm. The scarlet thread is placed upon Esau's toe, yet he will one day sell his birthright to be the grandfather of Yeshua, for a morsel of meat.

Boaz travels to the city gates where the elders of the community oversee transactions and covenants. He confronts the Jewish remnant at the gate and they deny their birthright to be the father of Messiah. The Pharisees and Sadducees were born.

Boaz removes his shoe and gives it to the nearer kinsman as his promise to redeem Naomi, Elimelech, to include his ancestral land in Bethlehem. I wonder if it is where Jesus Christ sojourned in a manger? Where did Ruth announce her intention to win the heart of Boaz. At Araunah's threshing floor. Have you won the heart of Jesus Christ?

Are you willing to enter Araunah's threshing floor, and kneel at the feet of Messiah? Jesus Christ is the lamb sacrificed on Araunah's threshing floor for the sin debt of all humanity. It is the same threshing floor where Ruth laid under the veil of Boaz, and Boaz promised to redeem her and Naomi. We are Ruth and Israel is Naomi. Jesus Christ died to redeem Israel and the gentile bride Ruth. Hallelujah!

How many people realize God went to extraordinary measures to redeem us to himself? The Bible in both Testaments is the only way to know if you are truly the virgin bride of Christ. The Book of Ruth is where we learn from God himself through the lives of ordinary people, how he would redeem mankind. Ruth willingly laid at the feet of Boaz. She humbled herself and crucified her past through the belief that Naomi's God would one day provide a lamb who through obedience to God the Father, receive a gentile bride. We are the virgin bride, betrothed to Messiah, awaiting his return to retrieve us as he builds our mansions in the fathers' house. The true doctrine of imminence!

Ruth became the ancestor of Mary, the virgin whom God chose to enter her womb, as the Son of God. Have you made Christ the Lord of your life? Adonai Elohim Echad Adonai! The Lord our God is one Lord!

Is Jesus Christ, the second person of the trinity, the Lord of your life, and do you acknowledge him as creator? Do you understand that the creator of the universe entered his creation in the womb of a virgin Jewish girl, to be born King of the Jew's.

To grow into Manhood and accept his mantle of Priest-King at his baptism in the Jordan.

To Be tortured by his creation and mocked by the false trials we subjected him to. We whipped him with 40- minus one lashes for the healing of the flesh. He then allowed us to mock him as he carried the cross up Calvary's lonely mountain.

Along the way only one Jewish man would help carry his cross. He then had us nail him to the cross of wood he prepared at creation in the garden of Eden. He watered that cedar of Lebanon for three thousand plus years. He had Pilate write his name above his head in all the languages of the Roman, Greek, and Hebrew world.

It was in Hebrew that he revealed who we had killed. Yehoshua Ha Nazarite,V Melek Ha Jehudim! Jesus Christ King of the Jews. As an acrostic, Yod He Waw He! YHWH Hallelujah.

He was crucified upon a cross of wood yet he created the hill upon which it stood!

RLTW John Burns 8-4-2021.

The Mark of Cain

Have you ever considered the story of Cain from a Hebrew hermeneutical perspective? His name transliterates as a man from the Lord. He was Eve's firstborn after the transgression, and the promised hope of messiah was first revealed as the plan of God.

Redemption has always been the plan. God is the God of creation. Creation required action. The action God planned is the most preposterous debt payment plan in Creation's History. It required God to enter the realm of His greatest creation, in the womb of a predestined Jewish virgin girl, as his own son, all for the purpose of redeeming man and creation to himself.

And the Word was preincarnate so God's plan has always been pre-incarnate. God does not react to anything or anyone. He is the God of Pre-incarnate action! Hallelujah.

No doubt Eve would have been thinking, my son Cain will be the father of the chosen messiah. Or maybe even from a religious perspective, he was that chosen messiah. The desire of every Hebrew woman is to be the mother of messiah.

Eve is the mother of all living. Is that from our perspective or God's perspective? A Hebrew is the descendant of Adam or his genealogy would not show up in the New Testament.

A Hebrew is the children of Abraham, Isaac and Israel (Jacob). Israel is comprised of all those humans who wrestle with God and wrestle with men. It was never meant to only become a national identity. The name of Israel was set apart, and reserved for all those born of a woman who would accept God's Messiah: The Lord Jesus Christ.

Today, the nation of Israel is on a collision course with Jesus Christ inheritance and their tribulation of the last times.

Israel will once again embark on building a home they believe can contain God. Their temple will end up being the Lord Jesus Christ temple after national Israel looks upon him whom they have pierced, and cry Hosanna, blessed is he who comes in the name of the Lord. They will finally recognize their risen Messiah and king.

The Star of David is actually the star of Messiah. It incorporates the first and last Passover lamb's blood in two right angle triangles.

At the first Passover in Egypt, Israel was commanded to smear the blood upon the lentil above the doorpost and upon both side doorposts. At the last Passover, God's lamb was slain with the Romans nailing his hands and feet forming another right triangle of the blood of the lamb.

The national symbol of Israel is the menorah. The menorah is the seven churches of revelation identified by Jesus Christ as the seven lampstands.

When the light is in heaven, the nation of Israel will suffer persecution. The rapture of the bride of Christ is fast approaching and Israel will lose their engrafted brothers on earth. They will be surrounded by all the nations' of the earth, that are intent on stopping God's plan. But that plan has always included the mark of Cain. Hallelujah.

According to scripture, Cain was firstborn so he alone would have enjoyed pre-eminence in the family. His mom was told the messiah would come through a virgin woman and the son would inherit everything. The birth of Cain would have pleased Adam. Adam was reeling from unbelief so no doubt he neglected to teach Cain proper rites for bringing an offering to God.

When Cain followed in Adam's foot-steps he became the gardener in the family. He would have toiled over his land, and no doubt would have felt the need to horde his crop. He must not of learned the law of tithing yet. If he had, he would have brought God the first ten percent. Instead, Cain brought God some of what was left over. Wrong move on Cain's part.

When Abel appeared with the firstlings of his flock of lambs, of course it pleased God. He always intended to slay a lamb to cover the sins of humanity. Abel understood this, and his offering was accepted. Cain let jealousy arise, and when he and Abel were in the field, he killed Abel, and buried him in the ground.

What was Cain thinking when God appeared and questioned him about Abel's where abouts?

The Mark of Cain

The God of creation who communes with mom and dad, is asking you where your brother is, and you get cynical? Strike Two.

God already knew Abel was dead. He wrote the script in eternity past. This is act two in God's profound cosmic love story. Eve's firstborn proves that sin exists to bend our knees toward God and his salvation. The mark of Cain proves it! Hallelujah.

Jesus Christ himself identifies as the Alpha and Omega. What he actually said in front of his Jewish audience of priest's was, I am the Aleph and the Tau. Like the Greek language, in Hebrew, these are the first and last characters in their prospective alphabets.

In Hebrew the Aleph is the Ox or burden bearer. That same Ox is also an animal of sacrifice. Which burden bearer became our eventual sacrifice? Who is the Aleph? Then who is the Tau.

It is the Last letter in the Hebrew Aleph-Beit. It is representative of the cross. It is the cross shaped letter in the Hebrew letter sequence. It was designed by God our burden bearer and messiah. That same God would eventually succumb to the Tau or cross. It was all part of his grand strategy.

God orchestrated every aspect of our lives, and the lives of every person born of a woman. Why do you think science uncovered that every photon knows where every other photon is located, in the entire universe, at all times'.

The same God created them all at his big bang when he appeared in our dimension of time as the light of the world. He is the designer of creation, He upholds creation, and he died to redeem Creation, Hallelujah.

What about the mark of Cain? What was it? I have heard countless gentile preachers go from tatoos to brands. Once again, I turn to Hebrew hermeneutics and equidistant lettering sequence in the closed loop system, we call our Bible.

The mark of Cain, it turns out, is the Hebrew letter TAU! God marked Cain with the cross.

What other sign, has God Given, beside the sign of Jonah?

Cain was born of a woman. He was born with the ability to follow God or lean to his own understanding. This is called Sin. No matter how you put it, Cain needed God's mercy and grace and what is the one mark in history which identifies God with these divine attributes? The answer can only be the Tau. The cross of Jesus Christ is what he marked Cain with.

Has God marked you with the cross of Christ? Do you pick up your TAU daily and follow Jesus Christ?

Would you show mercy and grace to Cain? How about mercy and grace to your wife or husband? Or children? We all need the mark of Cain daily.

Cain was God's second witness of the Cross of Christ in our Bible. The first was the tree of the knowledge of good and evil.

The Mark of Cain

God created a garden in which he intended to put you and me. He gave us every seed- bearing plant for sustenance, that we were to manage as his highest creation. He told us not to touch or eat the tree in the midst of the garden. It was Elohim's tree. He would bring that tree to fruition all by himself and it was to our benefit.

But we did what humans always do, question the authenticity of God's word. Did God say? Hell, we have created so many houses designed to question this very affirmation from God: His word.

We all need God's mercy and grace, and church needs it the most. The time has come for judgement to begin, and to begin in the house of God! Hallelujah.

Then God had humans tend the tree for 3000 years. He taught men to fashion incredible iron instruments of war. In his season, he had man fashion three iron nails and a long spear. I am that man. I bear the mark of Cain. I fashioned the nails and the spear.

Then God instructed me to hew down the tree and fashion it into the TAU! Then he had me spit on him, condemn him unlawfully, and eventually nail him to that TAU. And the entire time he opened not his mouth, for he planned it all in eternity past! Hallelujah.

Now the conclusion must be, that the mark of Cain, in whatever form the creator fashioned it to his head, was the TAU or cross of Christ. Humans have had no excuse. The

Cross has always represented God's mercy and grace, and his pattern has always been the Tau.

He said so himself. For Humans require the mercy and grace of God every day and no mark in history beside the Hebrew Tau, represents the mind of God like the cross of his Messiah son Jesus Christ.

I look forward to taking up the mark of Cain, and carrying it daily until my Messiah returns to rapture me home.

Even So Come Lord Jesus Christ.

He was crucified upon a cross of wood yet he created the hill upon which it stood.

RLTW John Burns 6-8-2020.

Where Metaphors Abound, Mysteries Reside! Dr. Chuck Missler. Well done Good and Faithful Servant.

The Two-Edged Sword

Revelation 2 provides insight into how Jesus Christ viewed God's word. It is he who said I have the sharp sword with two edges. It was Paul in Ephesians who reminds us to take with us the sword of the spirit which is the word of God. Has Jesus opinion ever changed as to the written revealed word?

What happened to the scripture that Paul gleaned his Gospel from in 1 Corinthians 15 Vs. 1-5? I believe Christian men became devoutly antisemitic to escape persecution. I believe they began to combine Greek gnosticism with the Roman fertility pantheon first begun in Babylon under Nimrod.

The rebellion by Romanized Christian preachers was a reaction begun in Pergamos when men married Christianity to the eugenic Greek mind in western Turkey. Their goal was to secure a hierarchy of elite preachers who held a monopoly on what God thinks. They were racist then, and they are racist now.

How you treat one Jewish King, and his brethren in the flesh, determines whether you are saved, sanctified, and eventually glorified in the coming kingdom of Yeshua ha Messiah.

Paul was raised in Tarsus, a Roman province in an extremely pagan Greek world. The Greeks were the original purveyors of the need for socio-political elite priests who controlled the flow of information about their god's, to the common Greek citizens.

To the Lord and to Christians, these men were the Nicaolaitans that Jesus Christ says he hates. They do what is right in their own eyes, and they lead people down the wide road that will lead to their eventual destruction.

The Nicaolaitans are a sect of confessing Christian's who combined the Greek pantheon of gods with a little bit of New Testament Jesus.

At Pergamos they allowed the worship of Ishtar to replace God's calendar established in the Old Testament. They replaced the 14th of Nisan as the date of the crucifixion, with a Roman calendar date of a Friday crucifixion. No way to get to Jesus Christ prophecy of being in the grave three days and three nights with a Friday crucifixion.

They replaced the resurrection, with the celebration of the bunny rabbit fertility goddess Ishtar. They gave it a Roman name: Easter. The golden egg of Ashtarte had migrated into church, and God is angry.

The resurrection occurred on the 17th of Nisan. Yet Christians blindly do what the men Jesus Christ hates continue to do. Make God a liar. They do not read the bible themselves and, they rely on Greek educated pastors to wrongly divide the word of truth.

To divide something, you need two things which God gave all of us. The old and new testaments. Yet, antisemitic men and women continue to lean only on New Testament grace, without going through Old Testament mercy. Blasphemy.

The word Nicaolaitans can be understood by its' English transliteration. It is gleaned from two Greek words. Nicao; To rule over. And, laity; the people.

Jesus Christ hates any kind of church hierarchy. Period.

He is the only mediator between God and men. He is the author and finisher of our faith. The anointing we receive from him is real not counterfeit, you do not need any man to teach you. The Holy Spirit was given at Christ ascension for the purpose of finding Christ a willing bride taken from men. One person and one confession of faith at a time. The Church has become a socialist mechanism for keeping government from persecuting people.

1 John 5;4 and a move away from Church attendance toward home groups for worshipping is the goal of Jesus Christ. That is where Paul, Peter, Jude, John, Matthew, Mark, Luke, Titus, and James the just met with Christians.

God does not dwell in houses made with human hands. He is the God of time while occupying all space.

Modern Christian preachers shame people into a false sense of salvation. This has been the pattern since Constantine first Romanized Christianity in 323 AD. Modern denominational Christians deny the Gospel to most of our sinful society. They kidnap God for set periods of time, judge others while never looking into the mirror to admit they have played a role in Americas' abandonment wrath of God.

They prostitute grace and never practice mercy. They believe God saved them to be societies judge of all things dealing with outward piety. They have no power, and Jesus Christ is no-where near their three- dimensional pagan temples.

Jesus Christ is standing at the door of their churches and knocking, which means he is outside.

Fear is the opposite of faith. Modern preachers keep their congregations in a constant state of fear because they are being paid to enlighten men to the marriage of church and state.

They have no idea who Jesus Christ is according to the Old Testament.

If they read the Old Testament, revival would never be needed for they would understand God would never build a house on any other foundation then those found in the Old Testament.

Modern preachers in America deny the irrevocable covenants found in our Old Testament. Genesis 12 promises how a believer can be blessed in God's eternal kingdom.

Genesis 22 is the akedah and the means by which God said he would be the lamb slain on Calvary.

2 Samuel 7:14 brings a believer behind the veil of eternity to explain that one day Jesus Christ would become the root and the offspring of King David. It is a future Kingdom of

Jew and Gentile to be established after the final 7 years of Gentile government on Earth.

Jeremiah 31;31 is the eternal covenant that explains how God always intended to pay the sin debt of humanity by Jesus Christ.

Without the knowledge of these covenants the New Testament is alone, and it leads to wielding only one edge of the sword of the spirit, denying Christ true identity, and leading to Christian confusion and a lack of power in their testimony.

Mercy is the story of the Old Testament in the lives of our Jewish ancestors. Grace is the revelation of Messiah with the continuation of monotheistic history in the gospel narrative. The Old Testament is the New Testament revealed, and the New Testament is in the Old Testament concealed. You cannot go through Grace's door without having Mercy's keys!

At the heart of this doctrine of replacement theology is antisemitism, the oldest form of racism on Earth.

Revival is needed in America but it will never come until preachers repent and return to Hebrew hermeneutics as taught by every writer of our New Testament.

Every word of the New Testament can be uncovered in the Old Testament, and true Christian doctrines can be understood only with proper Old Testament instruction.

It was Christ model for warning the Hebrews and it is my model for warning modern Christians that they are being led like sheep to a slaughter. Repent and return to the two-edged sword of the word of God, and your Christian testimony will become one where sick people are healed, dead people are raised incorruptible, and poor people receive riches unfathomable.

He was crucified upon a cross of wood, yet he created the hill upon which it stood.

Even so come lord Jesus Christ.

RLTW John Burns 7-28-2021.

Into the Breach

When I joined Bravo company 3/75, I had very little experience with demolitions. My level of competence ended at setting up the claymore mine. All that changed when I committed to becoming a Ranger leader.

First, I attended the demolitions MTT with instructors from within our company. We would go to the demolitions range and learn Ranger demolitions charges from a more offensive perspective. We would learn different charges designed for a specific mission tailored for the Ranger squad and fire team. We would learn defensive charges from the Abatis charge, designed to block roads using trees and telephone poles. We would learn charges to disable enemy vehicles. We would learn to employ Bangalore torpedoes for breaching wire obstacles. Everything needed to help a Ranger rifle squad complete the mission and bring success to our company.

When I became a Line Squad Leader in third platoon, emphasis changed to breaching doors, walls and windows in a complex MOUT environment. Military operations in urban terrain, is the acronym used to describe operating in a complex city environment. This requires surprise, speed, and violence of action.

Each demolitions charge was designed for specific mission capability. Most involved insertion by helicopter to a specific breach point. Both electric and non-electric means for initiating charges were employed, depending on time at the breach. I attended another MTT with only Squad Leaders form my company with instructors from JSOC at Fort Bragg as our mentors. This experience changed my entire focus as a leader, and made me realize that as a Ranger, life was getting incredibly more responsible.

I would deploy to Somalia in August of 1993 as Third Platoon Weapons Squad Leader. I would be responsible for deployment of my weapons squad in a means that required multi-tasking requirements. I had an incredible lot of men to deploy. Three machine gunners, three assistant machine gunners, ammo bearers and myself, with multiple missions of complex responsibility.

These men were incredibly talented and incredibly diverse. I was the least in this amazing squad of men God had entrusted me with, to persecute total war upon an enemy our President had chosen. Rules of engagement had to be ironed out in country.

Rangers are designed, trained, and mentored to LEAD WITH LED! Placing restrictions upon them in a time of war, is counter-productive to mission accomplishment.

One Mission I would draw in Somalia was to train demolitions engineers in the 10th Mountain about potential obstacles they may be required to attack while deployed to Somalia. These engineers were much more competent than I at removing barriers through demolitions, so basically, I shared with them what I had been taught by our Older Brothers in JSOC to tailor their attention toward the MOUT environment. Luckily, I had Timothy " Griz" Martin to help me prepare, and Dave Ritchie to actually teach them what they needed. I was just the observer who was learning as they were.

As weapons squad leader in Somalia, my primary mission was to oversee two vehicles in the assault force we had gathered for offensive operations. I would tactically cross-load my squad over three Jeep teams of HMMV's. I would have Dave Ritchie as My Gunner, Chad Fowles as my Driver, Clay Othic on the 50 Caliber, with Jason Dancy hitching a Ride with me or SGT Aaron Weaver as the other Team Leader in a two jeep Team. Sgt Lorenzo Ruiz was my number two in charge of my vehicle and its' daily mission deployment. Chris Schlief would join SSG Dave Wilson with Reese Teakel as His assistant Gunner. Dominic Pilla would be deployed as the Number One Gunner on Jeff Struecker's Team. Ed Kallman would draw the unfortunate Job as Driver for another team. Sandy Pursley would Join us in Somalia upon his completion of Ranger school.

I had an incredibly gifted talent lot to deploy. Somalia asked of Rangers what no previous deployment of men had required. Beside our primary mission of assault support for the task force, third Platoon would also be required to escort convoys through dangerous parts of the city. We would also pull our share of gate guard and constant defensive perimeter reinforcement. All while being on a short mission leash.

Luckily, we had two competent Leaders in Larry Moores and SFC Bob Gallagher our Pl and PSG respectfully. They would manage us the best they could to support the increasing amount of missions, that third platoon would draw while deployed. My weapons squad and third platoon as a whole would perform impeccably.

To give proper insight into the Ranger mentality and talent pool I must write about one incident in Somalia I am incredibly proud of my men for. Besides stealing the flag off the UN headquarters, my weapons squad were on gate guard. They spotted a large number of Somali men boarding a Russian plane on the tarmac. Our mission was to capture a Warlord and his chain of command who had been terrorizing the Somali population. He was responsible for the death of a Former Green Beret in December of 1992 and we wanted them prosecuted.

Larry Freeman and I shared common ground. We both were from Philadelphia. We both had Jewish blood running through our veins. We both loved our country. We would die for a cause bigger than ourselves. My cause was the men assigned to my left and right. Larry Freeman was killed trying to help Somalia escape Islamic terrorism.

On this day, my men decided to take initiative. They spotted men with funny shoes and Rolex watches boarding the plane. They came and got me so we blocked the plane from taxiing. We then proceeded to board the plane and request their Somali passports. Immediately the charade started. Men began crying and refusing to produce documents. So, we abruptly ended their flight and asked them to offload the plane. They were having none of it. So, Chris Schlief escorted one of them to the door and politely threw him down the gangway to the tarmac. The rest decided to deplane peacefully. We escorted them to our chain of command who turned them over to the UN authority.

I Have no idea what happened after that, but I was proud of my men for being incredibly alert. And they accomplished all this while not being distracted by the incredibly hot Russian women who were assigned as flight attendants on this plane. I was saddened by the fate of these stewardesses. I know at least one lost her job, because she showed up in a pornography movie in Weapons platoon after we redeployed to the states.

Back to the breach. Upon my return to Third Battalion after being injured in Somalia, I left Bravo company for The Special Skills shop. I would again attend a demolitions school to further my education on explosive theory. This involved a level of knowledge that surpassed my ability at the time. How-ever it lingers in my mind as I pen these words.

The men I attended this school with would go on to distinguish themselves in Iraq and Afghanistan as Operators of varying levels. All would be required to breach incredibly dangerous objectives. Some with helicopters, some on ATV's. All at incredibly sophisticated levels of precision. These men permeate my thoughts and these men are the reason I enter the hardest target rich environment of my career. Once again, God has allowed me to practice master breaching.

The hardest target I have ever prepared for is the heart of the American Special Forces soldier. From Ranger, to Green

Beret, To Seal, to Airforce PJ and CCT, and Marine Special Forces soldier. If not for the humility learned from Operator Dan Busch I would fail miserably, and failure has never been an option in my life.

There is a hostage crisis in America. It occurs every Sunday in Churches in America and around the world. They purvey in the message that Jesus Christ died to make bad men good. That is false! Jesus Christ Died to raise dead men to life. We are all spiritually bankrupt. Kidnapping God for two hours on Sunday will never fix the heart of the man.

Negotiating a proof of life by giving an offering of whatever is left-over, will only ever pay the preachers salary. Holding God hostage for set periods of time, and never releasing him back to our American communities is a heresy. God needs Rangers in heaven and on earth. This protracted war on terrorism has enlightened Americans to the plight of our soldiers when they return from war. I know. I have been coming home for 27 plus years.

The seeds planted in my life over time have caused me to realize that God is not done with me. He wants to use me just like I am. That means keeping everything I learned, and tailoring it to my new mission: Getting special people saved. I was one of those people: unless you asked Colonol James Jackson! He once said Rangers were not special, but I beg to differ. I have bled with men that he could never hold a candle to. These are the men God wants in his kingdom and he has once again sent me into the breach.

Baalim was riding his donkey going to curse God's covenant people. Baalim had been warned by God not to go. He tried through earthly means to negotiate with God. Just like we all do at set times: We negotiate with God.

God first sent an Angel to block Baalim's advance. He still would not listen. It was time for drastic measures. God opened the mouth of the donkey to speak to Baalim and warn him of his impending demise. I am the modern jackass God is using! America is on the doorstep of the abandonment wrath of God and he will have to judge America or repent and apologize to Sodom and Gomorrah!

I was an intemperate man in my youth. I did everything at 110 MPH. I never thought about consequences. Then I entered the Valley of Elah to face my giants without the stone which the builders rejected. I put on the world's armor to deal with my giants.

Alcohol, Narcotics, Women. I have tried them all. I have failed miserably at all three.

Then Jesus Christ got a hold of me. The seeds Dan Busch had planted in my life began to sprout when I realized my own insignificance in God's created world. I realized immortality could only be gained through surrender and not chaos. I would be required to surrender to the most preposterous debt payment plan in human history. The debt I owed was to none other than God himself and I alone could never pay it.

Outward Piety and religious conviction would never get me into God's kingdom. My entire way of thinking about God would have to change and if Jesus Christ is God, then he would be the one orchestrating the change.

What were the seeds Dan Planted in my life that I took for Granted for many years? Dan Busch told me he loved me in spite of myself. He told me it was not sin that separated me from my creator, it was how I went about covering my sin. Sin is the debt we are all born with as God's explicit image in creation. All have sinned and fall short of the glory of God. Sin is debt, and that debt had to be paid. God alone willingly paid it.

It all began in Eternity past when Lucifer led a rebellion in heaven and he and one third of the Angels who sinned with him were cast to the Earth. God had to create new worshippers on earth and he first had to make the earth inhabitable. The entire creation is created for your and my existence. God is in control and there is only global warming if God allows it.

The creative name of God is Elohim and it is the first mention of the trinity in the Bible. The trinity exists to pay your sin debt. Nothing but the death of God himself could ever pay your sin debt. God created us with the knowledge that we would sin. He did it to prove to Lucifer that he alone is God.

When God enables a sinner to become an overcomer, Lucifer loses a soldier! We become overcomers only when we believe in the death, burial, and resurrection of God's Son Jesus Christ. Jesus Christ exists as God and the son of God because he alone is God and no one but God alone could extinguish the sin debt we owe God.

This is a mouthful but it is a hard Truth. It takes a lifetime of repentance and requires we submit to God's mercy and grace daily. Relationship is the only requirement, and then, lambs become lions and God emerges victorious. Hallelujah.

Sin exists to prove to Lucifer that God overcame sin on Calvary's Cross. The entire Law with 613 commandments, exists to show us just how feeble and unable we are in this life without God's Grace. It is a free gift, and the only way it is earned, is by acknowledging that we exist in the presence of sin.

Justification is the first step to enter God's kingdom. It is imputed when we acknowledge our need for God's eternal mercy over our lives. Then grace appears in the form of Jesus Christ, and the Holy Spirit begins to sanctify us through the washing and cleansing of God's word. The only requirement is the faith to believe that God did it all alone to bring you into the kingdom of His son for all eternity.

I love My God. He is the Trinity of the entire Bible message. He came up with the most preposterous debt payment plan in history and he initiated that plan all by himself. The crucifixion was not a tragedy! It was the triumph of God over Lucifer's rebellion and we are just pawns in God's interstellar war! Choose this day whom you will serve; as for me and my house we will serve the Lord!

He was crucified on a cross of wood yet he created the hill upon which it stood.

RLTW John Burns 7-29-2021.

Special Operations Wounded Warriors

2016 was my official homecoming. The community I once served, was asking me to serve once more, but not before welcoming me home.

It had been twenty-three years since I returned from Mogadishu, Somalia injured. It had been a long time since I had toasted the men I lost, and brothers I never got to say goodbye to. This organization exists to find men like me. Brothers-in-arms who somehow got lost on the road after doing exactly what their creed requires. Somewhere along the way I had stopped Rangering. Or so I thought.

I was a United States Army Airborne Ranger. I spent five years in a Rifle Company in the 75th Ranger Regiment. I would dare to say the best Ranger rifle company the Regiment has ever seen. I was one bearing in the gears of Bravo Company that when in time, made the whole engine work. Bravo Company was home to me, and the men I served with are my family. The DNA that makes up our family, can never be manipulated. It is a blood covenant.

Rangers serve at the behest of the president. They are as close to tier one as any unit gets. While not always enjoying the budgets of other special operations units, no unit has been asked to do more for our country. And Bravo Company has led the way every time.

On Rio Hata in Panama, Bravo Company 3/75 lost SSG. Larry Bernard and Pfc. Roy Brown, with Bill Dunham and Patrick Kilgallen suffering injuries that still remind them each day of their sacrifice. These men are the reason I served.

I had the privilege of welcoming these men home from the hospital in 1990. I have remained a steadfast advocate for my brothers and my best friend in life served in their platoon in Panama. Paul Mercer is the greatest Ranger and best American I have ever met and called my friend.

I remained In B 3/75 for five years. I served in positions ranging from Mortar Section FDC Chief, Team Leader in a Rifle Platoon, Squad Leader of a Rifle Squad and culminating in my job in Somalia, Weapons Squad Leader, Third Platoon B 3/75 Rgr Regt. The greatest privilege the Lord Jesus Christ ever bestowed upon me was the privilege to lead Rangers in combat. Nothing since has kept my attention.

In Somalia I had an amazing group of men in my squad. My three machine gunners were all better than me at being a daily Ranger. Dominic Pilla, Chris Schlief, and Dave Ritchie are three amazing Americans. Dominic would die in Somalia leading with lead, and killing his killer. Chris Schlief was unwavering in Mogadishu, and the most brilliant man I have ever encountered. He has continued to serve our country in special operations and today he is A CSM in an SF Group. Dave Ritchie was my gunner on my vehicle on October 3, 1993. He is my hero. He was wounded early in the mission and continued to fight with an M16 after his Mg was disabled. Dave ended up leading our vehicle home when I was wounded near the front of the convoy for the third time. Dave was a Spec4 in Somalia. I had my gunner Clay Othic wounded seriously with the loss of his shooting arm. Lorenzo Ruiz took over the 50 caliber, and was fatally wounded taking over from Clay Othic. I was wounded once by gunfire early, and once by Shrapnel before I was hit the third time making my way back through the convoy toward my vehicle. That left a Spec4 in charge of my vehicle team, and the rear of the convoy. Dave Ritchie was able to lead them for two hours as we fought our way back to our base. Dave Ritchie would go on to serve in Task Force 160th as a CH 47 pilot for every year of the GWOT. He retired a CW4, and continues to serve his state as a pilot fighting forest fires in California. He is an American Special Operations hero.

Chad Fowles was an AG for Dave Ritchie and drove our vehicle. He somehow managed to not get hit in Somalia. God has a plan for Chad Fowles, and I pray SOWW helps him find it. Chad retired as a MSG with twenty years in the Army. Along for the ride on my vehicle was PFC Jason Dancy. He also managed to not get hit, but it does not diminish his contribution to the Regiment and Bravo Company lure. He fought like a Spartan on October 3, 1993. Reese Teakell was Chris Schlief's new ammo bearer in Somalia. His first deployment in Bravo Company was to Somalia. Reese went on to serve the Regiment after returning from Somalia in every position from team leader to squad leader to CSM of the Special Troops Battalion. He is today a CSM in a Brigade of the 82d Airborne division. Ed Kallman rounds out weapons Squad who fought on October 3, 1993. He was the driver for another vehicle and managed to not get wounded. I was privileged to lead these men in support of the Special Operations mission to Somalia. I intend to work tirelessly to bring these men home to SOWW and back together as a Ranger family.

I left the Army in 1995. I was a Platoon Sergeant in Vicenza, Italy. A final act of mercy from a loving God. I got to share with my platoon in Italy the lives of my squad, and their heroism in service to the Regiment and SOCCOM. I live every day for the chance to share my life and it's struggles with my Ranger brothers and SOWW is the platform that continues to make it possible.

As the country debates our nation's path forward, one thing that is undebatable. The true 1% of Americans that should be recognized are the 1% of Americans that have actually volunteered to defend the American life we enjoy on battlefields most Americans know not exist. When you break it down further, less than 1 tenth of 1% of those ever serve in a special mission unit. The freedom we all profess comes at a cost that continues to be paid for by the 1 tenth of 1% of Americans who get to call themselves the SOCCOM family. It is a family that can never be divided, and SOWW is the greatest mechanism for keeping the family recognized and together, as we embark on the next phase of our lives.

America has once again become apathetic to all things military. We can never surrender. If we surrender, this entire experiment of a government of the people, for the people, and by the people will perish from the earth.

SOWW exists to make sure America never forgets the lives led by Rangers, Seals, Operators, and Airmen, who continue to provide America with a blanket of protection. The freedom we enjoy is because of men who serve in SOCCOM. SOWW is the place where SOCCOM family reunions continue to occur.

I was privileged to meet a man I now can identify as my brother while attending a SOWW event in South Carolina. I was stepping out in extreme faith by attending this event. My Ranger brother, and survivor of Mogadishu, Dave Floyd had invited me to the annual SOWW hog hunt called Takin Bacon. I accepted and boy was God a gracious God. Not only did I connect with men I had served with, I got to meet an entire generation of special men who had now served our country in a protracted war with no end in sight. But one I will never forget. Eddie Oglesby was one of the dog handlers. I felt there was something more to Eddie so I struck up a conversation with him. Eddie had served our nation in Viet Nam as a Ranger in Papa Company 75th Infantry. He and I were DNA brothers, and we were meeting at SOWW. I sensed Eddie was experiencing his own sort of homecoming. SOWW was the mechanism by which Eddie and I connected, and we will be brothers who look forward to Takin Bacon every year. I miss Eddie every day. He taught me more about responsibility to my brothers than any shrink could ever hope to learn in twenty years of practice. SOWW did that for me and an old Ranger from Viet Nam who came home to a divided nation. Imagine the Rangers coming home now?

SOWW provides special men with the opportunity to share their experiences with people who will be able to show empathy rather than sympathy. The stories would never be understood by a public that has lost its sense of understanding toward freedom's high cost. Special Operations Wounded Warriors caters to the needs of men who have been wounded defending our ideals as Judeo-Christian Americans. Our creeds are our bond and promise to this nation. Our experiences in war are our bond to each other.

SOWW has put its money where its mouth is. Warriors from the SOCCOM community gather each year in March to fellowship, kill wild boar, and party like it's 1999. The place where this occurs cost money every year to lease. We at SOWW have been afforded the opportunity to purchase the property and make it a permanent destination throughout the year for men and families in our very small community who have borne the brunt of this protracted war on terror. It will never end, and our mission to our community will never end. Consider giving a monetary gift to further our mission from once a year to permanent status. The property along the river comes at a cost of three million dollars.

I know the Ranger community alone could raise that! This organization is limiting the damage to warriors in our community who need us to continue the family bonds on into eternity. We have borne the brunt of the freedom debt our country expects us to continue to pay. Please help us reach our goal.

Donations to our cause should be sent via www.sowwcharity.com. Please prayerfully consider helping our cause. It is our nations cause!

RLTW John Burns, He was crucified upon a Cross of wood yet he created the hill upon which it stood 6-9-2020.

A portion of the proceeds from the sale of every book will be donated to Special Operations Wounded Warriors in the name of Daniel D. Busch.

A portion of the proceeds will also go to Behind the Veil Ministries in the name of CW2 Aaron A. Weaver. My Ranger brother, an American hero, and a friend to all things Jesus Christ.

The rest of the proceeds will support Gold Star programs supported by the USSOCCOM community. We owe these family members continued support as they navigate this life without the brothers we served with.

Rangers Lead the Way!

Biography

John Burns is a staff writer at the Morgan County Today newspaper, the Chaplain of Special Operations Wounded Warriors non-profit, and the President of Behind the Veil Ministries Inc.

His Christian faith is the foundation for every aspect of his life. He is married to Susan C. Burns of Lancing, TN. He is blessed with four grown children; Sean, Andrew, Kasey, and Lisa. He also has eleven wonderful grandchildren.

His hobbies include; turkey hunting, hound dogs, hog hunting, beer tasting, coffee drinking, and studying the Bible every day.

His ministry to the special operations community was born out of his desire to serve the community that gave him so much in life.

"The men who came before me were giants. They led the way and ensured we would give it one hell of a go. I have so many to thank. The only way I know how is to serve them tirelessly so we can all fellowship forever on the other side of glory."

The road goes on forever, and the party never ends…

He was crucified upon a cross of wood yet he created the hill upon which it stood.

Printed in Great Britain
by Amazon